REVOLUTIONS and REVOLUTIONARIES

FOUR THEORIES

REVOLUTIONS AND REVOLUTIONARIES

BARBARA SALERT

ELSEVIER

New York / Oxford / Amsterdam

ELSEVIER SCIENTIFIC PUBLISHING COMPANY, INC.
52 Vanderbilt Avenue, New York, N.Y. 10017

ELSEVIER SCIENTIFIC PUBLISHING COMPANY
335 Jan Van Galenstraat, P.O. Box 211
Amsterdam, The Netherlands

Library of Congress Cataloging in Publication Data

Salert, Barbara.
  Revolutions and revolutionaries.

  Bibliography: p.
  1. Revolutions.   I. Title.
HM281.S29   301.6′333   75-40652
ISBN 0-444-99021-6

Manufactured in the United States of America
Designed by Loretta Li

To my parents

contents

ACKnOWLeDGmenTS

A critique owes its primary debt to the work it examines. I have learned much from the theories I have analyzed and, for this, I wish to thank their authors.

In writing this book, I have benefited from the helpful suggestions of many people. James Christoph, John Gillespie, Bernard Morris, and Frank Thompson read through numerous early versions—far more, I am sure, than they care to remember. Kenneth Auerbach, Mancur Olson, Jr., and Charles Ostrom read sections of the manuscript and helped to clear up several errors. At a later stage, Barry Ames, John Kautsky, and Merle Kling gave me invaluable aid, and I am grateful for both their criticism and their encouragement. Without the help of all of these people, this book could not have been written. Remaining errors of fact and judgment are, needless to say, my own.

I am also indebted to various people for their assistance in the preparation of the manuscript. Maryon Dunn typed the original manuscript and Lillian Ehrlich patiently typed the revisions. A grant for secretarial assistance from the Graduate School of Arts and Sciences at Washington University made it possible for me to obtain much of this help. Finally, I would like to thank my editor, William L. Gum, for his patient guidance.

St. Louis, Missouri
May 1976
                                        Barbara Salert

REVOLUTIONS AND REVOLUTIONARIES

I

INTRODUCTION

If importance is measured by magnitude of change, revolutions have attained an importance surpassed by few other political phenomena. The "great revolutions" of the modern era have had a tremendous impact not only on the daily lives of the literally millions of people involved but also on the course of history for decades to come. It is, perhaps, for this reason that the subject of revolution evokes an unusual emotional response. Men have pinned their hopes—and their fears—on the idea that, somehow, the social, economic, and political problems that face any nation will be resolved by a revolution. When such ideals as freedom, justice, and equality are at stake, it is not surprising to find people reacting strongly and somewhat less than dispassionately.

Under these circumstances, the high degree of interest shown in the phenomenon of revolutions becomes readily understandable. Since the changes wrought by revolutions affect virtually everyone in a society, the problem of revolutions is of general concern. Corporate executives become nervous when there is a student revolt or a ghetto riot, not because such incidents have any real effect on their position in society, but because they raise the specter of revolution. And, for their part, rebel leaders cheer such incidents because they, too, believe that these may contribute to the development of revolutionary movements. The strong emotional impact of even minor protest movements indicates quite clearly that when total upheaval is at stake, few people can remain neutral.

A simple emotional response to revolutions, however, means very little Those seeking to understand this phenomenon, as well as those who want some control over its development, need to know how such movements are forged and under what conditions they are likely to succeed in their objectives. Whether the end is to foster, prevent, or simply understand revolutions, then, the means must be the same: an analysis of the structural causes of these movements and the motivations inducing people to strive for their success.

Such analysis is not easy. People have long studied revolutions; we are still a long way from understanding this phenomenon in all of its ramifications. This is not due to any lack of insight on the part of the analysts, but to the fact that revolutions are highly complex events and their analysis must incorporate an understanding of numerous related phenomena. To understand why people participate in revolutionary movements, for example, we need understanding of the role of leadership in inducing participation, of the effects of socialization and the conditions under which people can radically change their belief systems, and of the nature of political violence in general. This means that to understand revolutions, we must also understand such diverse topics as political participation, socialization, and the role of leadership. This is clearly a task that cannot be accomplished easily.

To say that the task is difficult, however, is not to say that it should not be attempted. There have been literally hundreds of studies explaining revolutions and related manifestations of political violence. At this point, the literature in the field includes everything from detailed historical studies of particular revolutions to quantitative analyses of cross-national data.[1] These works, while perhaps not wholly successful, have nevertheless brought to light a

---

[1]Works on particular revolutions are by far the most numerous. These include such outstanding examples as Albert Mathiez, *The French Revolution* (New York: Grosset & Dunlap, 1964) and Robert Daniels, *The Conscience of the Revolution: Communist Opposition in Soviet Russia* (New York: Simon and Schuster, 1960). Cross-national studies are more recent but have also begun to proliferate. For a good example of this work see Douglas Hibbs, Jr., *Mass Political Violence: A Cross-National Causal Analysis* (New York: Wiley, 1973). There are also some excellent nonquantitative comparative studies such as Barrington Moore, Jr., *Social Origins of Dictatorship and Democracy* (Boston: Beacon Press, 1966). Other works in the field include

great deal of evidence and have provided a variety of insights about the nature of revolutions. And, it is from these works that we must ultimately extract the necessary information for constructing more adequate theories of revolution.

If existing studies are to serve as building blocks for developing better theories of revolution, it is essential to analyze both the contributions these studies have made and the defects in these studies that need to be corrected in subsequent work. Good theories rarely spring forth in isolation. Usually, the process of theory construction involves a long chain of development, modification, and reinterpretation of prior theories and hypotheses. This means that to formulate better theories of revolution, it is first necessary to carefully evaluate existing theories to discover which aspects of these theories require additional work.

Unfortunately, few attempts have been made to critically evaluate studies of revolution in some depth.[2] Thus, it is not at all clear how far existing theories have taken us nor what needs to be done to improve these theories. In this respect, the process of evaluation is as necessary to theoretical development as original research. If existing theories are not carefully analyzed and discussed by interested scholars, it is highly likely that subsequent efforts will suffer from the same problems faced by their predecessors.

The purpose here is to partially fill this gap in the literature by analyzing a selective number of theories of revolution. The particular theories that will be considered are those proposed by Marx, Johnson, Gurr, and Olson.[3] These theories focus on the two interrelated aspects of the revolutionary process that are of crucial concern to those who analyze this phenomenon: (1) the nature of participation in revolutionary movements, and (2) the social conditions affecting the likelihood that a revolution will occur in a society. These

studies of revolutionary leaders, such as E. Victor Wolfenstein, *The Revolutionary Personality: Lenin, Trotsky, Gandhi* (Princeton: Princeton University Press, 1967) and abstract theoretical works, such as Neil Smelser, *Theory of Collective Behavior* (New York: The Free Press, 1962).

[2]Some noteworthy exceptions are Michael Freeman, "Review Article: Theories of Revolution," *British Journal of Political Science*, 2:3 (July, 1972), pp. 339–59; Isaac Kramnick, "Reflections on Revolution: Definition and Explanation in Recent Scholarship," *History and Theory*, XI:1 (1972), pp. 26–63; Terry Nardin, *Violence and the State: A Critique of Empirical Political Theory* (Beverly Hills, Calif.: Sage 1971); and Lawrence Stone, "Theories of Revolution," *World Politics*, XVIII:2 (January, 1966), pp. 159–76.

[3]Marx's theory of revolutions is, unfortunately, scattered throughout various works. The basic texts that will be used include *Capital, The Economic and Philosophic Manuscripts, The Eighteenth Brumaire of Louis Bonaparte, The German Ideology, Manifesto of the Communist Party,* and various newspaper articles. The other theories are: Chalmers Johnson, *Revolutionary Change* (Boston: Little, Brown, 1966); Ted Gurr, *Why Men Rebel* (Princeton: Princeton University Press, 1970); and Mancur Olson, Jr., *The Logic of Collective Action,* rev. ed. (New York: Schocken Books, 1971).

two issues are probably the most fundamental ones in the study of revolutions, since the answer to other questions raised in such studies is at least partially dependent on the solutions to these basic problems. For example, those interested in knowing how to develop revolutionary movements need to understand what prompts people to join such movements. Similarly, to understand the consequences of revolutions, it may well be necessary to understand the causes of these phenomena. In other words, to understand various aspects of revolutions, we must (at least) understand the nature of revolutionary participation and the social causes of the occurrence of revolutions.

There are, of course, a variety of other theories that attempt to answer these questions. While the choice of using certain theories, to the exclusion of others, is neither easy nor completely justifiable from an analytical perspective, some selection of this nature must be made. At this stage, an overall survey of the literature is simply not useful. To gain any insight into the problems of formulating theories of revolution and some possible ways of solving these, an in-depth examination is required; this, in turn, means that the analysis must focus primarily on only a few theories.

The problem then becomes one of choosing those theories that most readily illustrate the general state of the field. This requires, I believe, that such choices be made in the light of two major considerations. The first is that, as far as possible, the theories should not be "straw men"; that is, they should be among the best examples of this type of theory. There is little point in analyzing problems that can be—and have been—readily solved. Analyzing problems that have beset even the best efforts in the field, however, may facilitate efforts to solve these. For similar reasons, one may impose a second constraint: that the theories selected represent different perspectives on the study of revolutions This allows us to distinguish general problems in the study of revolutions from those that only arise within particular perspectives. Furthermore, it serves to minimize the type of exaggerated concern with certain aspects of the revolutionary process that is likely to arise if the topic is viewed from only a single perspective.

The above theories satisfy both of these requirements. All have received widespread and serious consideration from social scientists, indicating they are viewed as major works in the field. While there are undoubtedly different opinions about the relative merits of these theories, few people would deny that they are among the top contenders. If they are "straw men," then, it is likely that every other theory of revolution falls into this category as well.

These theories also represent a variety of approaches and techniques that have been used to study politics in general and revolutions in particular. Gurr and Olson fall into what is generally termed quantitative political science.

Marx and Johnson, on the other hand, represent the nonquantitative perspective. In terms of the way approaches to the study of politics are commonly delineated, these theories represent the social-psychological, economic, Marxist, and functionalist approaches to the study of revolutions. And, since most theories of revolutions rely on one or more of these approaches and use the same basic techniques used by the above theorists, it is safe to assume that much of the analysis of these four theories could be extended to other studies of revolution as well. At the very least, it is highly likely that the types of problems that beset these theories are common to many other theories as well.

The Meaning of "Revolution"

One of the problems that is immediately gleaned from an analysis of these four theories—as well as from any overall survey of the literature on revolutions—is that there is no consensus about the object of study; that is, there is no single definition of "revolution" that is adhered to by all analysts. This means that general theories of revolution may not be at all comparable since these may actually be analyzing different sets of events. It is possible and, in fact, is frequently the case that an event constituting a revolution in one theory may not be considered revolutionary in others.

There is, however, overlap in conceptions of revolutions. Some events are universally recognized as revolutions, while others are virtually always excluded from this category. For example, all analysts treat the French and Russian Revolutions as "revolutions," whereas none include U.S. electoral changes as such. The basis for this overlap appears to be that all analysts share a somewhat vague conception of revolutions as structural changes in a society. Disagreements about the set of events denoted by this term arise partly from different definitions of "structural change" and partly over the nature of the other attributes that should be used to characterize the term revolution.

On a formal level, we may view the structure of a society as a set of simultaneous equations characterizing the way in which economic, social, and political resources are allocated in the society.[4] Structural change would then involve any change of parameters or any change in the form of the relationships among the variables used to characterize the system. On this

---

[4]This follows the standard definition of political systems as ones that involve the "authoritative allocation of values in a society." For a discussion of this see David Easton, *A Framework for Political Analysis* (Englewood Cliffs, N.J.: Prentice-Hall, 1965), pp. 47–57.

conception, "structural change" becomes precisely defined in theoretical terms. However, since a formal characterization of an entire political system is almost impossible to derive with any degree of validity, it becomes exceedingly difficult to use this definition to isolate those events that should be included under the category of revolutions. Without having numerical values for the parameters of the relevant equations, it becomes impossible to tell whether such events as the advent of Allende in Chile or the formation of the U.S. "welfare state" did or did not involve structural change.

Given this problem, it is probably advisable to return to the earlier and far more vague conception of structural change as any widespread social change. Note, however, that these two conceptions of structural change are not equivalent. On the formal definition, it is quite possible that there be widespread social change within a given structure. This might occur if the system's environment changes radically. In this case, the values of the systemic variables might undergo great changes—indicating widespread social change—but the structure of the system, or the way in which resources are allocated, would remain unchanged.

Although the basic idea of treating revolutions as events initiating widespread social change is probably quite acceptable, there is an obvious problem with this definition: it does not indicate how widespread change has to be for a given set of events to be a revolution. Events, such as the Chinese Revolution, that introduce changes in everything from the educational system to land-tenure patterns, clearly qualify as revolutions under this definition. But there are many changes of government that have been accompanied by a degree of social change that, while far surpassing routine reform, has nevertheless fallen short of the degree of change produced by such events as the French or Russian revolutions. The Bolivian Revolution of 1952 is one example of this; there are many others.

Further problems in defining "revolution" arise from the other attributes—if any—that should be used as defining characteristics of the term. Three such attributes seem particularly controversial: success, violence, and participation. The first raises the issue of which events constitute the revolution: the development of a revolutionary movement, the government takeover, or the transformation of society. This issue is probably less important than the others since if "revolution" is to refer to structural change in a society, that is, the actual transformation of society, it is nonetheless possible to speak of movements aiming for this goal or the overthrow of existing governments by such movements. Nevertheless, confusion sometimes arises over whether a successful revolution is one that succeeds in gaining power or one that succeeds in transforming society. It is equally unclear whether an unsuccessful revolution is a "revolution" or simply a "rebellion."

The other two attributes—violence and participation—are even more controversial. The "great revolutions," such as the Russian and French Revolutions, have involved both widespread violence and mass participation. This does not mean, however, that either constitutes a defining characteristic of "revolution." If a revolution is simply structural change in society, then either a coup or a peaceful election result might initiate a revolution. Nevertheless, many people would argue that a coup should not be counted under the label of revolution even if it initiates structural change in a society. Similarly, others would argue that "revolution" should be reserved for those events involving widespread violence.[5]

On one level, the confusion over the term revolution is easily resolved. A word may be said to mean what it is defined to mean, and if there are different definitions of "revolution," this simply means that the word is used to refer to different types of things. So long as the different meanings are not confused, one might reasonably claim that no problem arises. Confusion over the meaning of "revolution," in this view, should not hamper the development of adequate theories of revolution. The theorist need only choose his preferred definition and proceed with the task of analyzing the nature of those events denoted by the term.

On another level, however, this solution simply begs the question. A definition allows us to group different things under a single label. It asserts, in effect, that these things are similar. But similarity lies largely in the eyes of the beholder. We do not observe revolutions; we observe events, such as the storming of the Bastille or the armed clashes of the Zapatista rebels. These events are certainly different in many respects: they occurred in different countries at different times under different social conditions. They are also similar in some respects: they both involved the protest of lower-income groups against the existing government. The issue, then, is not whether these events are similar in any absolute sense, but whether they are similar in certain relevant senses, where relevancy is determined largely by theoretical considerations.[6] If a theory is designed to explain the "revolt of the masses," the two events might well be put together in the same category. If a theory is designed to explain urban revolts, they had best be kept separate.

This conception of definitions allows us to consider problems posed by multiple definitions of the term revolution in a somewhat different fashion.

---

[5]This is particularly, although not exclusively, true of cross-national studies, in which revolutions are taken to be extreme manifestations of political violence.
[6]For a more systematic analysis of these issues see Carl Hempel, *Fundamentals of Concept Formation in Empirical Science* (Chicago: University of Chicago Press, 1952), and "Fundamentals of Taxonomy," in *Aspects of Scientific Explanation and Other Essays in the Philosophy of Science* (New York: The Free Press, 1965), pp. 137-54.

The fairly common conception of revolution as structural change in a society may be used as an admittedly vague but nonetheless useful definition of the object of inquiry. In terms of a first approximation, such a definition will at least provide some common ground for further discussion. Any detailed analysis of this phenomenon, however, requires a far more precise conceptualization of the term. At this stage, the existence of multiple definitions becomes analytically justifiable. Since there are many different theories of revolution, and since these isolate different types of factors to explain this phenomenon, it is not surprising that there are a variety of different definitions of "revolution." In fact, given the theoretical relevance of definitions, such differences are probably unavoidable in any field of inquiry for which there is no single commonly accepted theory.

This means, though, that any analysis of the term revolution is limited utility. After the term has been defined in a broad sense, the focus of inquiry must shift from definitional to explanatory and theoretical issues. The important question becomes: "Which theory supplies satisfactory answers to the questions we have about revolutions?" rather than "Which definition of 'revolution' should be adopted?"

The Study of Revolutions.
Theories and Approaches

Within the past ten to twenty years an increasing amount of research in political science has been carried out under the rubric of some broad "paradigm" or "approach," which provides (or is intended to provide) the analyst with a definite perspective on the nature of politics and political behavior. The approach focuses the analysis by specifying assumptions about the types of variables and/or relations among these that are relevant to political analysis. When these assumptions are clearly formulated and fairly restrictive, they constitute, so to speak, the "core" of a theory and can be an invaluable aid in the task of theory construction.[7]

It is true, of course, that all theories rely on explicit or implicit assumptions, regardless of whether or not they are self-consciously based on some larger approach. In this sense, an approach (or paradigm) may be viewed simply

---

[7]The basic notion of a "core" of a theory and a research program to guide the development of that core has been set forth by Imre Lakatos, "Falsification and the Methodology of Scientific Research Programmes," in *Criticism and the Growth of Knowledge,* ed. by Imre Lakatos and Alan Musgrave (London: Cambridge University Press, 1970), pp. 91–195. Needless to say, the type of research program envisaged by Lakatos is far more specific than any of the approaches used in political science.

as a specification of a coherent set of assumptions. This, in itself, however, may be useful for any type of inquiry. Since all theories are based on assumptions, the theorist cannot decide whether or not to use assumptions, but he can decide which particular assumptions seem to be most appropriate for his inquiry. There is, of course, no reason for anyone to have to rely on some particular set of assumptions that constitutes one of the standard approaches. Nevertheless, these approaches do assure at least a minimal amount of coherence. Furthermore, by specifying the nature of the assumptions in some detail, the use of standard approaches helps the analyst to avoid relying on implicit or vaguely defined assumptions. The use of a standard approach, in short, can help the analyst to focus his inquiry with some degree of precision.

Once a particular set of basic assumptions has been chosen, a variety of theories can be constructed by adding hypotheses to the basic "core" assumptions. Theories can then be modified by changing one or more of these added hypotheses. This means that the task of constructing theories by building on the results of previous theories may be greatly facilitated by the use of standard approaches. If a group of theorists agree on the core assumptions that are applicable to some field of inquiry, the task of constructing improved theories becomes one of changing hypotheses outside this core. In this way, the approach facilitates efforts at revision by restricting the number and types of initial modifications. It indicates, in effect, that if a theory is unsatisfactory, the first type of revision that should be considered is one that leaves the core assumptions intact.

If this type of revision fails or seems infeasible, an approach may still be useful in suggesting alternative types of revision. In many cases, a broad approach does not consist of a single set of basic assumptions—rather of various sets of related assumptions. This means that there are often a variety of related theories and/or basic assumptions that become "obvious" choices to try if a theory is to be modified. Thus, even if the core assumptions of a theory seem to be unworkable, the approach may suggest ways of slightly altering these assumptions to obtain more fruitful results.

These issues may perhaps be clarified by a brief examination of one approach that is receiving increasing use in the study of politics: rational choice theory.[8] This approach focuses attention on the choices people make as they engage in political behavior. It assumes, in effect, that politics can be viewed in terms of the results of choices made by individual political actors.

---

[8]For an overview of the literature using these basic assumptions in the study of politics, see William Riker and Peter Ordeshook, *An Introduction to Positive Political Theory* (Englewood Cliffs, N.J.: Prentice-Hall, 1973).

The basic assumption of this approach is that when faced with a choice of alternative courses of action, people will choose that course of action that maximizes their expected utility. To put this less formally, the approach assumes that people make choices on the basis of what they take to be their self-interest.

Such an approach can obviously be used as the basis of a variety of theories of political behavior by adding hypotheses about the particular types of alternatives available and the nature of the participants in particular political processes. In studying voting behavior, for example, these hypotheses would include such things as the number of alternative parties, the effect of an individual's vote on the outcome, and the effect of the act of voting itself on a given individual.

If a theory of this type proved to be inadequate, one might first investigate the possibility of modifying the additional hypotheses. For example, if the original theory assumed that people derive no satisfaction from the act of voting itself, one modification would be to hypothesize that in advanced industrial democracies, in which people are socialized to believe that voting is a duty of citizenship, the act of voting will be a source of some degree of psychic gratification. This type of modification would constitute a plausible revision of a very simple theory of voting behavior.

A second type of modification would be to consider alternative assumptions that involve some modification or reinterpretation of the concept of rationality. In this case, there are a variety of modified rationality assumptions, ranging from "satisficing" behavior to probabilistic choice models, that might replace the maximization of expected utility assumption as the core of a theory of voting behavior. If the initial attempt to revise the additional hypotheses fails, it may be possible to develop better theories of voting behavior by reinterpreting the concept of rational choice.

There is, of course, no guarantee that any of these procedures will generate theories that are considered good or even adequate by people who study a given subject matter. Furthermore, these procedures are often difficult to carry out. If a theory uses a wide variety of hypotheses in addition to the core assumptions, it may be extremely difficult to determine which of these should be modified and how they should be modified. In general, the approaches that are most useful in both focusing a particular study and suggesting types of modifications are those that are based on fairly specific and restrictive assumptions. This means, though, that in order to gain the benefits of working within a well-defined approach, the analyst may have to rely on assumptions that may be too restrictive for a given line of inquiry.

The above considerations suggest that the choice of whether or not to rely on a standard approach as well as the choice of the specificity and strength of the assumptions that are to be used in a study involves some trade-offs. Reliance on a standard approach helps the analyst to focus his theories and allows a group of scholars to gain the benefits derived from sharing a common language and set of assumptions. In particular, it facilitates the task of theory construction by both restricting the nature of initial revisions and suggesting alternative routes of investigation. At the same time, approaches are restrictive, and approaches that are highly developed are often based on assumptions that seem unreasonably strong when applied in certain contexts.

The theories of revolution to be discussed here are based on standard approaches to the study of politics, but the specificity and strength of the underlying assumptions vary widely. While some theories rely on formalized and restrictive assumptions, others use assumptions that are less specific, but probably easier to accept. Olson's theory, for example, relies on the rational choice assumptions discussed above, in conjunction with the economic theory of public goods. These assumptions allow Olson to derive a fairly tight argument about the nature of collective action in general. It then becomes a simple matter to extend this argument to the case of revolutionary action or participation in revolutionary movements. The assumptions in this case are sufficiently restrictive to allow Olson to derive a reasonably precise theory of mass political behavior. On the other hand, the assumption that mass political action is based on rational calculations may be questionable, especially in the context of revolutionary movements.

In terms of the strength of the underlying assumptions, Johnson's theory probably lies at the other end of the spectrum. Johnson merely assumes that political change can be viewed in terms of systems analysis. This means that political change can be analyzed by considering the social conditions related to such change, without explicit reference to the individual behavior that is presumably responsible for the occurrence of these conditions. Johnson further assumes that political systems are homeostatic, that is, they have some feedback mechanism that allows them to react to changes in order to preserve the basic features of the political system.[9] Such assumptions, while probably easy to accept, are not very powerful, which makes it difficult for Johnson to derive a well-specified theory from these assumptions. Johnson, in short, relies on assumptions that are more plausible than those used by Olson, but the gain in increased plausibility also involves a loss of specificity, hindering the task of theory construction.

---

[9]This type of system is discussed in Easton, *Framework for Political Analysis.* For a modified conception see Walter Buckley, "Society as a Complex Adaptive System," in *Modern Systems Research for the Behavioral Scientist,* ed. by Walter Buckley (Chicago: Aldine, 1968), pp. 490–513.

Marx and Gurr rely on assumptions that are in between these two extremes. Marx's core assumptions are probably more restrictive than Gurr's but possibly less restrictive than Olson's. Marx assumes, in effect, that social change occurs as a result of the dialectical interaction between the way in which goods and services are produced in a society and the social and political constraints placed on this process. At the individual level, a similar assumption is made: people change their behavior and attitudes as a result of the interaction between their activity and consciousness of this activity, where activity is measured largely in terms of work or productive activity. These assumptions are more restrictive than the ones used by Johnson in that they specify components that enter into the basic relationships relevant to political change. At the same time, the components themselves are broad enough to encompass a wide range of behavior and attitudes.

Gurr's theory is based on social-psychological assumptions. These relate individual discontent to the discrepancy between the individual's perceptions of what he feels legitimately entitled to attain and what he feels capable of attaining under the status quo.[10] Since such perceptions can obviously be affected by numerous other factors, including tactical considerations, this assumption is not very restrictive. Nevertheless, it does focus the analysis on a particular type of process and thereby channels a theory of revolutions in certain directions.

Since the task of an approach is to facilitate theory construction, there is no way to evaluate the relative merits of these approaches without evaluating the respective theories. However, once these theories have been analyzed, it is possible to arrive at a tentative judgment about the feasibility of working within each of these approaches. In particular, once the areas in which a theory is defective have been discovered, it becomes possible to determine whether the approach can indicate feasible ways of correcting these defects. This type of analysis must be highly tentative since, to some extent at least, it involves speculation about the outcome of projects that have not yet been undertaken. Nevertheless, if our goal is the formulation of adequate theories, an evaluation of existing approaches may be a useful tool when used in conjunction with an evaluation of related theories. It allows us, in effect, not only to determine where existing theories fall down but also to gain some perspective on the types of issues that might feasibly be tackled and the types of theories that might be most useful in serving to construct better theories of revolution. In short, while the task of theory evaluation is basically negative, an evaluation of the underlying approaches in conjunc-

---

[10]This assumption is closely related to the frustration-aggression hypothesis in psychological theory.

tion with an evaluation of these theories can be used for highly constructive ends.

Theories of Revolution: Criteria for Evaluation

Theories serve a variety of functions, and there are numerous standards that may be applied to judge the extent to which any theory adequately fulfills these functions.[11] Any evaluation of a theory's utility, then, can only be made with respect to some particular purpose that the analyst wishes the theory to serve. It is entirely possible that a theory that is highly inadequate with respect to one possible function may be very good when evaluated with respect to another possible function. For example, a theory that provides a good explanation of some type of behavior might nevertheless provide no policy implications for dealing with this behavior in some desired way. The first task in evaluating theories, then, must be to determine the particular function that will serve as the basis for the evaluation.

Since the theories under consideration all share the common goal of attempting to explain revolutions, the analysis here will be limited to an examination of the proposed explanations; that is, theories will be evaluated only with respect to the adequacy of their proposed explanations and not with respect to any other function that a theory of revolutions might serve, such as providing a guide for revolutionary action. This limitation was imposed both because the theories themselves seem to be primarily concerned with the task of explaining revolutions and because political scientists are generally more interested in explanations than in any other use a theory might have.

There are, of course, numerous different criteria for adequate explanations. It is clearly impossible to evaluate an explanation without relying on certain standards of explanatory adequacy. On the other hand, it is obviously undesirable to attack a theory on the grounds that it fails to satisfy criteria that are themselves inadequate. If the task of evaluating theories is to have any use at all—in the sense of helping us to develop better theories—the evaluation must be made with respect to criteria that seem reasonable and desirable ones for theories to satisfy and that conform to the type of explana-

---

[11]For a basic discussion of some of the major views of theories see Ernest Nagel, *The Structure of Science* (New York: Harcourt, Brace and World, 1969), pp. 106–52. A more detailed exposition of different kinds of explanation may be found in Robert Brown, *Explanation in Social Science* (Chicago: Aldine, 1963) and Daniel Taylor, *Explanation and Meaning: An Introduction to Philosophy* (Cambridge: Cambridge University Press, 1970). The standard view is that theories should serve explanatory and/or predictive functions. There are, however, many different types of explanations that could be provided by a theory. Furthermore, in the social sciences, theories might also be evaluated in terms of their usefulness as guides to social action.

tion the theory offers. It makes little sense, for example, to evaluate a theory of the origins of the Russian Revolution by using standards that require the explanation to be applicable to all revolutions. If the latter standards are insisted upon, the explanation of the Russian Revolution need not even be examined since it will surely be found inadequate in all respects.

The criteria for adequate explanations that I use were chosen with regard to the above considerations. They constitute, I believe, a model of the type of explanation that all of the theories under discussion are attempting to provide. The criteria are also fairly weak ones if compared with standards of adequacy proposed by many philosophers. The reason for this is that the study of revolutions is at an elementary stage. People have some ideas about the types of factors that affect revolutions, but the relative importance of these factors and the way in which they are interrelated remain unsolved issues. Furthermore, due to a variety of problems—including the scarcity of data and the difficulty of formulating precise definitions of key theoretical concepts—progress in this field is likely to be slow. While it is certainly inadvisable to ignore such problems, it is self-defeating to expect theories of revolution to overcome all of them at this stage. It seems far better to judge the theories by criteria that do not require all that might be hoped for in a theory than to impose standards that, at this stage, would be impossible for any theory of revolutions to meet.

The model of explanations that will be used in evaluating theories of revolution is essentially a modified version of the statistical-relevance conception of explanations developed by Wesley Salmon.[12] According to this view, an explanation for the occurrence of a particular event or type of event consists, basically, in finding all those factors (and only those factors) that are known to be relevant to the event, in the sense that the presence or absence of these factors affects the likelihood that the event will occur. Ideally, the explanation will also indicate how each of the relevant factors is related to the particular event by stating the conditional probability that the event will occur, given the relevant factors.[13]

---

[12]Wesley Salmon, "Statistical Explanation," in *Nature and Function of Scientific Theories*, ed. Robert G. Colodny, (Pittsburgh: University of Pittsburgh Press, 1970), pp. 173–231.

[13]Formally, Salmon ("Statistical Explanation" pp. 220–1) characterizes an explanation sketch of the fact that x, a member of reference class A, exhibits attribute B in the following way:

$$P(A.C_1,B) = p_1$$
$$P(A.C_2,B) = p_2$$

where $A.C_1, A.C_2, \ldots, A.C_n$ is a homogeneous partition of A with respect to B

$$\cdot$$
$$\cdot$$
$$\cdot$$

$p_i = p_j$ only if $i = j$

$$P(A.C_n,B) = p_n$$

x is an element of $A.C_k$

The requirement that explanations specify the conditional probabilities of the events to be explained given all the relevant factors is a laudable but, for our purposes, overly restrictive goal. If this requirement is imposed, virtually no theory of revolutions can satisfy it. Consequently, only a milder requirement will be imposed: that theories specify the relevant factors and the type of relationship that holds between these factors and the event being explained.

The difference between these two requirements is quite simple. Under Salmon's formulation, an explanation for the occurrence of a revolution would consist of empirical laws concerning the probability of a revolution, given the relevant antecedent conditions. Theories of revolution, however, do not generally permit the formulation of such precise laws. For the purposes of this essay, all that will be required is that the theory stipulate the conditions affecting the likelihood of revolutions and whether these conditions increase or decrease (or are related in some more complicated way to) the likelihood of a revolution occurring.[14]

An explanation that merely fulfills this criterion, however, might be inadequate. Some factors that are relevant to revolutions in the sense that they affect the probability of revolutions occurring might nevertheless be of little value in explaining revolutions. The basic problem that arises is the need to eliminate spurious factors from explanatory accounts. A factor may be said to be spurious to the occurrence of an event if the observed association between it and the event is thought to be accidental rather than involving a "genuine" or causal relationship. To use a time-honored example, barometer readings are associated with the occurrence of storms; nevertheless, barometer readings do not cause storms. In this case, barometer readings are simply a spurious factor reflecting the causal association between atmospheric pressure and storms.

Salmon proposes to solve this problem by using what he terms a "screening-off rule." This requirement would exclude as spurious any variable that is found to be merely "symptomatic" of another.[15] Thus, in the above example, barometer readings would only be considered relevant to the occurrence of storms if atmospheric-pressure conditions were not taken

---

Note: A reference class A is homogeneous with respect to B if every property that partitions the reference class into subclasses is statistically irrelevant to B in A. A property C is statistically relevant to B in A if $P(A.C,B) \neq P(A,B)$. Any property that is not statistically relevant in this sense is, by definition, statistically irrelevant.
This explanation sketch is reprinted with minor modifications, from *Nature and Function of Scientific Theories* edited by Robert G. Colodny by permission of the University of Pittsburgh Press, ©1970.

[14]Some of the theories discussed are also concerned with explaining participation in revolutionary movements. In this case, the analogous condition would be that the explanation specify conditions relevant to revolutionary participation and how these affect such participation.

[15]Formally, D screens off C from B in A if

$$P(A.C.D,B) = P(A.D,B) \neq P(A.C,B)$$

Note that this condition actually follows from the conditions for explanations listed in footnote 13.

into account. Atmospheric pressure, however, is known to be a relevant factor and, under Salmon's relevancy requirement (discussed above), must be taken into account. Once atmospheric pressure is included in the explanation, barometer readings will no longer be considered relevant since the likelihood or probability of a storm occurring, given atmospheric pressure, is not affected by barometer readings.

The use of a screening-off rule of this type presupposes data that can be subjected to either experimental or statistical control techniques. Even if such data were available, it would often be difficult to apply this rule.[16] In dealing with theories of revolution, the problem is further complicated by the fact that many are amenable to neither experimental nor statistical controls. In general, then, the use of a screening-off rule will simply not be feasible.

The problem of possibly spurious factors is admittedly difficult to handle adequately. It is quite true that the assessment of spuriousness is often based on empirical grounds and involves the type of control procedures that would be used to ascertain whether Salmon's screening-off rule holds. Nevertheless, in the absence of effective procedures of this sort, there is another way in which spurious factors might be eliminated from explanatory accounts. This is through the use of a theoretical explanation that can account for the proposed relationships between the relevant factors and the event to be explained.

Normally, if some association between two or more variables is postulated, there is some plausible reason why this association should hold. It is often the case that a theory is questioned precisely because there is no explanation of how one event or type of event caused another. If it is possible to explain how some variable operates as a causal factor, there is good reason to believe that the variable is not merely spurious. This is most simply done by describing the mechanisms or processes underlying the associations predicted by the theory.[17] Instead of requiring the type of empirical justification for the inclusion of relevant variables proposed by Salmon, then, the procedure here will be to require a theoretical explanation—involving the mechanisms by which one variable operates on another—for the associations postulated by the theory.

---

[16]If we relied on this criterion, we would be faced with a rather severe problem of ascertainability in the case that the two variables C and D were identically distributed. Furthermore, it is highly unlikely (at least when dealing with messy social-science data) that $P(A.C.D,B)$ will ever be exactly equal to $P(A.D,B)$. In other words, reliance on this criterion to ascertain spuriousness may not be possible even if we are working with data amenable to this type of treatment.

[17]This is weaker than the usual formulation requiring that associations or laws relating two or more variables be explained by deducing the laws from other sets of laws. For a discussion of the deductive viewpoint, see Hempel, *Aspects,* pp. 343–45 and Nagel, *The Structure of Science,* pp. 33–37.

The two criteria that have thus far been imposed do not guarantee an adequate explanation: these criteria alone would make it possible to judge an explanation to be adequate, even though every statement in it were false! On common-sense grounds, such a situation is clearly absurd. Consider, for example, the following explanation: John Jones joined a revolutionary movement because he ate cream cheese, and all people who eat cream cheese join revolutionary movements. Many people would undoubtedly protest—and rightly so—that they had eaten cream cheese but had not joined a revolutionary movement. The objection here is that the explanation should not be accepted because it consists of statements that are not true.[18]

This situation is most commonly avoided by requiring that the statements constituting an explanatory account be true or confirmed.[19] Such a requirement, if satisfied, would ensure that proposed explanations consist only of statements that are accurate, at least to the best of our knowledge. For our purposes, however, such a requirement is unnecessarily strong. Theories of revolution pose difficult problems of testability, and it would simply be impossible, at this stage at least, to test all of the statements that form part of an explanation of revolutions. But this does not mean that all efforts to ensure some "empirical accountability" in our theories need to be abandoned. An easier and, from the point of view of the social sciences, more realistic requirement of empirical adequacy is simply to require that the theory as a whole be confirmed by available evidence.

There is a significant difference between obtaining confirmation for every statement that constitutes part of an explanation and obtaining some confirmation for the theory as a whole. The latter criterion is much weaker than the former. It requires, in effect, only that some statements of an explanation, or some derivations of these statements, be confirmed. While some evidence in favor of a theory as a whole is not as satisfactory as evidence supporting every part of an explanation, there seems to be no way in which theories of revolution could reasonably be expected to fulfill the latter requirement. For this reason, all that will be required is that the theory be testable and confirmed by the available evidence. This requirement is by no means easy to satisfy, and most theories of revolution run into trouble at this point. Nevertheless, without some (albeit weak) confirmation requirement, any explanation satisfying structural requirements may be deemed adequate even though it bears no relation whatsoever to the "real world." This situation is so

---

[18]This explanation could also be discarded on the grounds that there is no theoretical linkage between rebellion and eating cream cheese. The "explanatory factor" is probably spurious.

[19]For a concise discussion of the distinction between truth and confirmation requirements see Wesley C. Salmon, *Statistical Explanation and Statistical Relevance* (Pittsburgh: University of Pittsburgh Press, 1971) pp. 105–10.

undesirable that it seems justifiable to impose a confirmation requirement even though it is very difficult for theories of revolution to satisfy even weak requirements of this sort.

The standard "hypothetico-deductive" account of confirmation requires that theories be tested by examining empirical evidence that would confirm or disconfirm observational consequences deduced from the theory. Thus, from the theory and certain "auxiliary hypotheses" that specify, among other things, the measuring devices to be used, certain predictions about the course of events in the real world are derived.[20] If confirmed, these predictions provide evidence in support of the theory. However, if the predicted consequences of the theory turn out to be false, the theory itself is disconfirmed or, at any rate, found to be inadequate in this area.

This account is highly oversimplified. There are, in the first place, several variants to the above account. For example, predictions might include statistical predictions about classes of events. Or, it might be required that the "confirming instances" used to provide support for a theory be "properly selected" in some specified sense. For the purposes of this study, statistical evidence will be admitted. However, no requirement on the distribution of historical case evidence will be imposed since this type of evidence is generally difficult to obtain, and more stringent requirements would rapidly eliminate any possibility of obtaining such evidence for or against a theory.

Furthermore, neither confirmation nor disconfirmation is as mechanical as the above account would indicate. A single confirming instance does not, of course, confirm a theory. It probably makes little sense to speak of any precise point at which a theory may be deemed adequately confirmed. Nevertheless, we would clearly want to test our theories under a variety of conditions before judging them to be "well supported" by empirical evidence.

However, a false prediction will hardly serve to refute totally a theory. The failure of a predicted consequence may be blamed on one or more of the auxiliary hypotheses rather than the theory itself. Or, it might be argued that the required boundary or antecedent conditions were not met and the test was therefore invalid. Even if these techniques fail, all a false prediction will show is that there are some "anomalies." These are not likely to overthrow a theory unless a better alternative theory can be found.[21] If a theory can successfully predict in some areas, it is better than no theory at all, and should not be discarded merely because it has "problems" in other areas. Testing procedures, then, are not really designed for the purpose of refuta-

---

[20]These predictions, of course, do not have to be predictions about the future course of events. They may simply be predictions of statistical regularity.
[21]For a discussion of this, see Lakatos, "Falsification."

tion per se. They are, rather, designed to reveal the problematical aspects of theories.

One of the major problems of the social sciences—if not *the* major problem—is the difficulty of testing predicted consequences of theories. In the social sciences there are generally no auxiliary hypotheses that would be commonly accepted as "unproblematical" background knowledge. If the predicted consequences of a theory fail to obtain, then, there is little way of deciding whether to blame the theory or the auxiliary hypotheses. This problem might be partially solved by trying a variety of plausible auxiliary hypotheses. If the predicted consequences fail to obtain under all of these hypotheses, there is good reason to suspect that the problem lies with the theory rather than the auxiliary hypotheses. In many cases, however, theories fail under some, but not all of the different auxiliary hypotheses used. In this situation, social scientists face the difficult task of evaluating the relative merits of the alternative hypotheses.

Further problems of testability arise from the types of predictions that social-science theories are capable of generating. Generally, predictions in the social sciences cannot be disconfirmed. Most social science predictions are surrounded by a *ceteris paribus* clause or boundary conditions that are rarely, if ever, realized. It is usually possible to argue that the predicted consequences of a theory failed to come about because the relevant boundary conditions were not met.

A similar problem occurs when predictions take on the form of probabilistic statements about classes of events. In principle, statistical inference could then be used to test these statements. However, it is often the case that the data being used do not meet the assumptions required for statistical tests. Thus, it could always be argued that a particular statement was rejected because background assumptions were not met.

These problems are severe and cannot be solved in any completely satisfactory manner. Most of the theories in political science fall short of desirable standards of rigor and precision and are generally supported by evidence that is, at best, problematical. But problematical evidence is better than no evidence at all. Under these conditions, it is reasonable to adopt a somewhat tolerant attitude toward testing procedures, which means that in some cases it may be necessary to relax some assumptions or neglect some boundary conditions, a situation not desirable. It seems, however, that for now it is the best.

Theories of revolution face all of the problems described above. In addition, they are beset by problems that make it particularly difficult to adequately test these theories, foremost among which is the problem of definitions. Many of the concepts used in theories of revolution—such as "revolution," "legitimacy," "alienation," and "dissynchronization"—refer to complex and multifaceted phenomena that elude precise definitions. Problems with theoretical definitions of "revolution" have already been noted,[22] and similar problems occur with many other concepts used in theories of revolution. These terms also generally lack precise specification of empirical referents; that is, it is almost never clear exactly what phenomena in the real world are to count as instances of the term. This clearly presents problems in testing theories since it is obviously difficult to test a hypothesis concerning the causes of revolution, for example, if it is not known what events in the real world constitute a revolution.

The severity of this problem, however, should not obscure the fact that even definitions that are not precise may be quite adequate for many purposes. It is often possible to divide events into those falling under the purview of some concept, those lying outside of the set of events denoted by the concept, and "borderline" or ambiguous cases. Of course, if a definition is so imprecise that virtually every case falls into the borderline category—that is, if it is hardly ever clear whether the term may or may not be applied—we will be "in trouble." But, this situation does not occur very often. Although the problem of definitions is undoubtedly a serious one, I am not convinced that it is insurmountable or that every theory of revolutions must founder on this rock.

Finally, theories of revolution suffer from data problems. Revolutions, however these may be defined, are not particularly common events. The lack of a great amount of data on revolutions is not terribly problematical for theories that are fairly broad and cover other phenomena, such as civil violence, as well. However, a theory that purports to deal only with revolutions, may face severe testability problems due to a paucity of data.

Furthermore, the type of data on revolutions that is available to us is often not reliable. Social scientists rarely witness a revolution; they rely on participants' descriptions of what took place or subsequent historical analysis. Both are likely to be incomplete accounts. While a revolution is in progress, people are not concerned about data collection, and even if they were, the confusion that ensues from revolutions would inhibit the collection of reliable data. Then, too, revolutions tend to be viewed in highly emotional terms, and probably more so than in many other areas of inquiry, "facts" tend to be confused with "values."[23] Subsequent analysis must therefore rely on data that are probably incomplete and possibly biased.

---

[22]See above, pp. 5–8.

[23]One could, of course, argue that no data are free from distortions because observation is always "theory-laden," that is, our data always depend on the particular theoretical perspective being

Data problems definitely limit prospects for testing theories by examining a wide range of consequences. It is obviously impossible to test a theory if no empirical evidence is available. Generally, however, some data are available that could be used to test some of the predicted consequences of a theory. Some of these data may be highly suspect. In this case, every attempt should be made to rely more heavily on tests based on more reliable data. In the final analysis, however, all we can do is base tests on the best available data. So long as it is recognized that the results of such tests are tentative and may be overturned by subsequent tests, it is far more satisfactory to require theories to be subjected to empirical tests than to allow theories to be deemed adequate even though they are supported by no empirical evidence.

Given all the testability problems facing theories of revolution, a requirement of empirical support cannot be too strong. Nevertheless, it does seem reasonable to require that theories at least be testable; that is, that they be expressed in such a way that some evidence, if available, would either support or fail to support the theory. Furthermore, the predicted consequences of theories of revolution should be supported by some empirical evidence. This evidence may take the form of statistical studies or historical case studies. In either case, the available evidence should not contradict the theory.

In summary, the criteria to be used in evaluating theories of revolution are as follows: (1) The theory should stipulate which factors are relevant to revolutions; (2) an explanation of why or how these factors are relevant should be provided; and (3) the theory should be testable and confirmed by the available evidence.[24] These conditions are not easy to satisfy. Nevertheless, as indicated above, they represent weakened versions of requirements commonly imposed on theories in the philosophical literature. Given the state of political science in general and the study of revolutions in particular, satisfaction of these weakened criteria is about as much as can realistically be hoped for.

There is probably no theory of revolutions that completely satisfies even the weakened criteria being used here. However, the use of these criteria should permit us to evaluate how far these theories have taken us and what aspects of these theories require further research and development. Furthermore, depending on the specificity of the approach underlying the theory, it

---

used. This may well be the case. Nevertheless, some types of observations strike us as being more problematical than others, possibly because there is no common consensus about the theoretical perspective underlying these observations.

[24] Implicit in the testability requirement is a definitional requirement: At least some of the concepts used in a theory must have empirical import, in the ordinary sense of the word.

may be possible to specify more precisely the assumptions or hypotheses that are in need of revision. Finally, it may be possible to arrive at some tentative judgments regarding the feasibility of working within each of these approaches by examining the kinds of modifications that would be required if the theory were to satisfy all of the above criteria for adequate explanations. The evaluation here is only tentative; hopefully, however, it will heighten our understanding of the study of revolutions and perhaps even facilitate subsequent research by pinpointing fruitful avenues that require further investigation.

▌▌
THe rational Basis OF revolutionary action

People do not typically join revolutionary movements. The average person today will probably live without ever engaging in revolutionary action. Even those who are caught up in a revolutionary situation are likely to become revolutionaries for a limited period of time, if at all. The professional revolutionary, in short, is a rare creature.

This situation is not surprising. Even though poverty and social injustice are rampant throughout most of the world, the average person is likely to accept his "fate" in life as natural and, to a large extent, beyond his control. The thought of a revolution will either not occur to him at all or else will be quickly dismissed as an unattractive alternative. For one thing, people are socialized into believing that the existing order is just, and these beliefs are not likely to change without a great deal of provocation. And even those who feel that their plight is unfair may well decide that, in the face of government opposition, revolutionary action might be futile. Those who participate in revolutionary action, after all, run the risk of not only losing their own lives but possibly also of endangering the lives of their friends and relatives. People are not likely to be willing to take such risks for a cause that may fail. Revolutionary action, in other words, is probably rare because people either do not want a revolution or because they are not willing to pay the cost of a revolution or both.

In spite of these obstacles, however, there have been some people, in a wide variety of societies, who have tried to make a revolution. Most such attempts have been failures. Nevertheless, in some cases revolutionary movements have succeeded in attracting large numbers of people to their ranks. These cases have often, although not always, culminated in the success of the revolutionary movement. They also provide us with incontrovertible evidence that, despite all the reasons why it should be difficult to elicit popular support for revolutionary movements, people do participate in such movements and, in some cases, even determine their success or failure.

Yet, it is not at all clear why this phenomenon should occur. Participation in revolutionary movements is relatively rare, and people who do participate in such movements must surmount serious obstacles. Why, then, do they engage in revolutionary activities? This question is crucial to an analysis of revolutions since revolutions clearly will not occur unless people decide to make them. But, the answer to this question is far from obvious, and there have been many different attempts to try to solve this problem.

Generally speaking, explanations of individual participation in revolutionary movements are framed within one of two major perspectives: the psychological and the rational. The psychological orientation focuses on the frustrations that cause people to deviate from their normal routine and rebel against the existing political order. This type of explanation will be examined later. Here we will focus exclusively on an attempt to explain participation in revolutionary movements as a rational choice of the participants.

The rational-choice explanation of revolutionary action is highly controversial, if only because it is so counterintuitive. It attempts, in effect, to disabuse us of the notion that people participate in the actions of revolutionary movements because they want the revolution to succeed. Instead, the basic contention of the rational-choice explanation is that people participate in revolutionary movements because they derive some personal gain. Unless such gains are provided, people will not join revolutionary movements. Since revolutionary movements do not often have the resources needed to offer personal gains to prospective participants, revolutionary action is likely to constitute a rare type of event. Thus, the theory of rational choice explains both why people engage in revolutionary action and why such behavior is infrequent.

The basis of the rational-choice explanation of participation in revolutionary movements is set forth in Mancur Olson's general theory of collective action.[1] A brief overview of this theory and its relevance to the study of revolutions will be presented in the following section. To evaluate this explanation, however, a more precise formulation is needed. This requires a careful consideration of the concept of rationality that forms the core of the theory. Once this concept is explicated, it is easy to develop the rational-choice explanation of revolutionary participation in a relatively rigorous fashion. This allows us to pinpoint possible areas of theoretical problems and to evaluate the theory in light of historical evidence. In this way, it is possible to assess the plausibility of the theory in view of both theoretical and empirical considerations.

Revolutionary Action as a Rational Choice

The basic assumption of Olson's theory is that people act rationally. In other words, a person who is faced with alternative courses of action is assumed to choose the alternative that he thinks will best further his own interests. The rational individual, it should be noted, need not be selfish; his interests may well include considerations of the welfare of others. For example, a rational person may desire a revolution because he feels that most people in his society would be better off under a revolutionary regime. All that is required is that he act in a way that is expected to satisfy his desires to the greatest extent possible.

With this assumption in mind, Olson then considers what happens to groups that attempt to provide a "public" or "collective" good. This type of good is characterized by the fact that if it is provided for anyone in a given group, it cannot be feasibly withheld from the other members of that group.[2] Generally, any group that attains a common objective is providing a public

---

[1]Olson, *The Logic of Collective Action.* Unless otherwise specified, all references to Olson refer to this work.

[2]Strictly speaking, public goods are generally defined in terms of two characteristics: (1) jointness of supply and (2) nonexcludability or external economies. "Jointness" means that a unit of the good can be made at least partially available to more than one person. "External economies"—the characteristic referred to above—means that at least some of the benefits of the good cannot be feasibly withheld from any individual in the group. For a more elaborate discussion of the concept of a public good, see John G. Head, "Public Goods and Public Policy," *Public Finance,* 17:3 (1962), pp. 197–219. Olson defines a public good solely in terms of nonexcludability, and this usage will be followed here. Revolutions, however, fall under what Olson has termed inclusive collective goods, and these, by definition, exhibit a considerable degree of jointness. Thus, revolutions are a public good by either definition.

good for members of that group. For example, if a country has an adequate system of national defense, the benefits (or lack thereof—public goods may also be public "bads") of national defense cannot be withheld from anyone living in that country. Similarly, if a revolution succeeds, all people in a given society will be living under the new regime. Those who did not want the revolution in the first place cannot simply choose to follow old laws and leaders. Those who favored the revolution cannot be denied the benefits of living under what they might view to be a more equitable social system.[3]

If we accept the view that revolutions do, to some extent, at least, provide public goods, it becomes very easy to derive Olson's major conclusions by simply applying the well-known "free rider" problem in the theory of public goods to the case of revolutions.[4] This problem typically arises when the group of people interested in the public good is quite large. In this case, the contributions of any single individual toward supplying the public good may be expected to be small—so small, in fact, as to be virtually negligible. For example, the average potential revolutionary probably expects to have very little impact either on the probability of the success of the revolution or on the nature of that revolution. He will not expect the revolution to fail if he does not participate and succeed if he does. If this is the case, the individual is in a situation in which, given the nature of public goods, the probability of his receiving the good (in this case, the results of a revolution) is not dependent on his actions.

Let us further suppose that the only relevant considerations in the individual's decision as to whether or not he should participate are the extent to which he values a revolution and the risks he expects of incurring certain "costs," such as death, imprisonment, or loss of a job, if he participates. If the individual does not like the idea of incurring these costs, then if he is rational, he should not join a revolutionary movement. For if he does, he may suffer the undesirable costs of such participation; if he does not, he will still receive the same benefits he would have received had he participated. The individual, then, has nothing to gain from participation but much to lose. In this case, his rational course of action is "to stay at home, keeping out of it."

This analysis may, of course, be extended to cover any case in which a group of individuals share common interests that can be attained through collective action. The analysis, thus far, would indicate that on the assump-

---

[3]It might be the case that all people who did not wholeheartedly participate in the revolutionary cause would be shot or suffer some similar misfortune if the revolution were to succeed. In my opinion, this tactic is highly infeasible. Nevertheless, this and other forms of coercion will be treated as "selective incentives." For the moment, it is assumed that no such exclusionary device is expected.

[4]For a lucid discussion of this problem, see James Buchanan, *The Demand and Supply of Public Goods* (Chicago: Rand McNally, 1968), pp. 77–99.

tion of rationality, such collective action should not occur. How, then, can we explain that collective action does occur fairly frequently? Olson's answer may be understood by relaxing two of the assumptions of the above analysis: that the actions of an individual do not have a noticeable effect on the supply of the public good and that the only relevant considerations are the extent to which the individual values the public good and the costs he expects to incur if he participates in the collective action.

The breakdown of the above two assumptions allows us to postulate the conditions under which an individual might be expected to participate in some form of collective action. The first (and for our purposes, far more important) condition occurs when private goods (goods for which exclusion is possible) or "selective incentives" are attached to the public good so that the individual cannot obtain the private good unless he simultaneously helps to provide the public good. In this case considerations other than the value of the public good presumably enter into an individual's decision, and he will engage in collective action if he feels that obtaining the private good is sufficiently important so that he would be better off if he had the private good even though he paid the costs of collective action. These selective incentives may be of two types: private inducements and negative sanctions or coercion. The first would include such things as the expectation of a high office should the revolution succeed or, possibly, psychological gratification.[5] The second would include physical violence or the threat of similar sanctions should the revolution occur.

The second condition under which a public good may be provided occurs when an individual's actions have a noticeable impact on the chances of the public good being supplied. This condition is likely to be of greater importance in analyzing coups rather than revolutions but may perhaps be used to explain why certain leaders choose to engage in revolutionary action. It seems reasonable to assume, for example, that such people as Lenin and Mao did believe that they could significantly affect the course of the revolution. If we accept Olson's theory, it is relatively easy to account for the participation of a few outstanding revolutionary leaders. What becomes difficult to explain is the voluntary participation of the masses. In fact, if we rule out ideological or psychological factors, as Olson seems quite willing to do, it would seem that in the absence of coercion, a mass revolution should almost never occur.

One might, of course, object to this theory on the grounds that people do not, in fact, behave in this manner. But there are certain situations in which

---

[5]Olson seems to believe that emotional or ideological factors will generally not be sufficiently strong to serve as selective incentives (Olson, pp. 12–13). This, however, is an empirical question and one that will be considered later.

people do appear to behave in a way that is consistent with this theory. Consider, for example, the case of the typically conservative U.S. businessman who supports increased defense spending. In spite of the fact that a large percentage of his taxes will be spent on defense, the man will probably try to find every loophole available to avoid paying taxes. In fact, the very prevalence of coercive measures to enforce tax payments leads one to suspect that if taxes were collected on a strictly voluntary basis, there would be no government. For a similar example, one might note that discussions of a volunteer army are almost invariably accompanied by arguments for increasing the pay scale and other private benefits that a soldier would receive. Apparently patriotism alone is not considered to be a strong enough force to lead people to voluntarily devote several years to "their country's service."

One or two examples, of course, will in no way indicate the adequacy of a theory. These examples, however, can be readily multiplied to explain such diverse phenomena as closed-shop practices among unions and disproportionate spending in international organizations.[6] It seems, then, that there are at least some types of situations in which people do behave in a manner consistent with the theory. Before drawing conclusions about the relevance of this theory to the study of revolutions, we must, of course, examine both the theory and the evidence in greater detail. The very general outline of the theory presented above, however, does seem to indicate that we cannot simply dismiss the theory on the grounds that people do not behave in this way: it appears that they do, at least in some cases.

The above considerations place Olson's theory in a somewhat advan-

---

[6]For a discussion of these, see Olson, pp. 66–97 and Mancur Olson, Jr., and Richard Zeckhauser, "An Economic Theory of Alliances," *The Review of Economics and Statistics,* 48:3 (August, 1966), pp. 266–79. Other scholars have largely limited their tests of Olson's theory to the cost-sharing arrangements in international organizations. These groups are generally "privileged" in the sense that one member, usually the United States or the Soviet Union, has a disproportionate interest in the public good and would presumably benefit even if it had to supply the entire good by itself. In such groups the public good will largely be provided through the efforts of the major party since once that country has provided its desired amount of the good, the other countries in the alliance have more than enough. These studies are limited to small organizations such as NATO and WTO and will not be analyzed here since they are largely irrelevant to the analysis of revolutions. For a review of these studies, see Frederick Pryor, *Public Expenditures in Communist and Capitalist Nations* (Homewood, Ill.: Richard D. Irwin, 1968), pp. 84–127; Bruce M. Russett, *What Price Vigilance?* (New Haven: Yale University Press, 1970), pp. 91–126; and Jacques M. Van Ypersele de Strihou, "Sharing the Defense Burden Among Western Allies," *Yale Economic Essays,* 8:1 (Spring, 1968), pp. 261–320, as well as the Olson and Zeckhauser article cited above. For an additional test of Olson's theory, see Philip M. Burgess and James A. Robinson, "Alliance and the Theory of Collective Action: A Simulation of Coalition Processes," in *International Politics and Foreign Policy,* rev. ed., ed. by James N. Rosenau (New York: Thre Free Press, 1969), pp. 640–653. It should be noted that none of these tests provides unambiguous support for the theory.

tageous position in that it is useful whether or not we find it applicable to the case of revolutions. If evidence about revolutionary situations indicates that the theory does provide an adequate way of viewing this phenomenon, we have the advantage of a theory that can help explain revolutions. However, even if the evidence is totally negative, Olson's theory raises some questions that are, I believe, fundamental to an analysis of revolutions. The most important of these concerns the location of the apparent difference between revolutionary situations and those situations where the theory does seem applicable. If we find that revolutionaries, unlike taxpayers, do seem to be able to engage in collective action without the aid of selective incentives or differential benefits, the most obvious question to ask is why does this distinction occur? In particular, we would want to know why the free-rider problem would not arise in revolutionary situations. And any theory of revolutions that purports to explain revolutionary participation on the basis of a (possibly different) conception of rationality will have to come to terms with this problem. In other words, even if Olson's analysis is totally inapplicable to revolutionary situations, it may provide a useful contribution to the study of revolutions by suggesting some definite avenues of investigation that need to be pursued, at least if we wish to remain within the rational-choice framework.

The Concept of Rationality

Before analyzing Olson's theory in greater detail, it may be useful to consider the conception of rationality on which the theory is based. Although Olson never explicitly discusses the concept of rationality, he does indicate that he is using the usual economic version. In this view, a rational individual is one who acts as if he were trying to maximize his expected utility.[7] We will consider here the case of an individual who is faced with the choice of alternative courses of action. Each of these actions may result in a number of different outcomes. A rational individual is expected to be able to evaluate

---

[7]We assume here that individual preferences can be represented by a real-valued utility function. There are certain regular types of preferences, such as those that are lexicographically ordered, that cannot be represented in this way. The maximization of expected-utility hypothesis, however, need not depend on a real-valued representation of utility, although the discussion below will assume this representation. For a discussion of the application of the maximization of expected-utility principle in which preferences may be ordered lexicographically, see John Chipman, "Non-Archimedean Behavior Under Risk: An Elementary Analysis—With Application to the Theory of Assets" in *Preference, Utility, and Demand*, ed. by John Chipman, Leonid Hurwicz, Marcel Richter and Hugo Sonnenschein (New York: Harcourt Brace Jovanovich, 1971), pp. 289–318.

his preferences for each of these outcomes in relation to the others.[8] He may not, however, know which of these outcomes will occur under any given course of action.[9] In this case, the individual must choose a course of action without knowing what the outcome will be.

Under the conception of rationality commonly used by economists, the individual in such a situation will choose the course of action that yields the highested *expected* utility, where the expected utility of any action is the sum of the individual's valuations of the possible outcomes multiplied by the probability that these outcomes will occur if the individual adopts the given course of action.[10] This, of course, assumes that the relevant probabilities of the various outcomes occurring are known or can be estimated. At the outset we will assume that this is the case. (In a later section we will consider the case in which some of the relevant probabilities cannot be estimated.)

To simplify matters and to make the discussion consistent with Olson's theory, our analysis will be couched in the form of cost-benefit calculations rather than direct expected utility maximization. In this type of analysis, the various "costs" and "benefits" (as perceived by the individual who must choose a course of action) associated with any particular outcome are sepa-

---

[8]The discussion here is highly oversimplified. The maximization of expected utility hypothesis used in economic theories of choice under risk is actually based on a number of rather restrictive assumptions concerning individual behavior. Since these assumptions both imply and are implied by the maximization of expected-utility hypothesis (assuming also that the usual axioms of probability theory hold), it may be useful to state these to see why this conception of rationality has come under heavy attack.

The formulation used here follows Milton Friedman and L. J. Savage, "The Expected-Utility Hypothesis and the Measureability of Utility," *The Journal of Political Economy*, LX:6 (December, 1952), pp. 463–74. Start with a situation in which the number of outcomes is finite (and, strictly speaking, "sufficient"). The individual chooses among alternatives (or "lotteries") that consist of probability distributions over various outcomes. It is assumed that the preferences of individuals for these alternatives are determined only by the probabilities and the possible outcomes, so that the form of the lottery is not significant. The notation $f \leqslant g$ means that alternative f is not preferred to alternative g. The postulates underlying the maximization of expected-utility hypothesis, following Friedman and Savage, are: (1) For all f,g,h, (a) $f \leqslant g$ or $g \leqslant f$ and (b) if $f \leqslant g$ and $g \leqslant h$, then $f \leqslant h$ (2) If $af + (1-a)h \leqslant g$ for all a such that $0 \leqslant a < 1$, then $f \leqslant g$ (3) For $0 < a < 1$, $af + (1-a)h \leqslant ag + (1-a)h$ if and only if $f \leqslant g$.

Various objections to these are discussed by Alex C. Michalos, "Postulates of Rational Preference," *Philosophy of Science*, XXXIV:1 (March, 1967), pp. 18–22, and Amartya K. Sen, *Collective Choice and Social Welfare* (San Francisco: Holden-Day, 1970), pp. 94–99.

[9]We do assume, though, that there is some "state of the world" under which a particular action has a certain outcome and that there is a probability distribution (which may or may not be known or meaningfully estimated) over the various possible states of the world. If the probability distribution can be estimated, the choice situation is one of "risk"; if it cannot, the situation is one of choice under "uncertainty."

[10]Strictly speaking, any interpretation of probability consistent with the axioms of probability theory may be used. For a discussion of the maximization of expected utility hypothesis under different interpretations of probability, see H. E. Kyburg, Jr., "Probability and Decision," *Philosophy of Science*, 33:3 (September, 1966), pp. 250–61. In this essay the usual practice of adopting a subjectivist interpretation will be followed. Specifically, "probability" is taken to refer to the individual's beliefs regarding the likelihood of particular outcomes.

rated. The individual is then assumed to choose the course of action that yields the maximum expected net gain, where the net gain is equal to the value of the benefits minus the value of the costs. The use of cost-benefit analysis is somewhat undesirable since if it is to be consistent with the maximization of expected utility hypothesis, additional restrictions must be made on the nature of individual-choice behavior.[11] For our purposes, it is sufficient to note that we must assume that for each outcome there is some function that can be used to transform units of benefits into units of costs, independent of the actual magnitude of the costs, and that the value contributed by each of the benefits (or costs) does not depend on the level of the other benefits or costs. For example, a person's valuation of a revolution is assumed to be independent of his valuation of his own life. The only grounds I can see for adopting this assumption is that if we are willing to make it, the analysis of collective action is quite simple; if we are not, it is rather complicated.

To avoid possible misgivings at this point, I should point out that the assumption of rational behavior does not mean all men are expected to think in these terms or to actually perform any of the above calculations. All that is

---

[11]For a complete discussion of these, see Peter Mark Pruzan, "Is Cost-Benefit Analysis Consistent With the Maximization of Expected Utility?" in *Operations Research and the Social Sciences*, ed. by J. R. Lawrence (London: Tavistock Publications, 1966), pp. 319–35. Here, the results will be summarized for the case in which an outcome or "state of the system" can be represented by a vector $(x_1, \ldots, x_m, y)$ in which y represents the costs. The conditions listed below apply to all such vectors. It is assumed, as usual, that to each state there is an associated utility $v = u(x_1, \ldots, x_m, y)$. Consider now the case in which the vector is of the form (x, y). The yx space is represented as

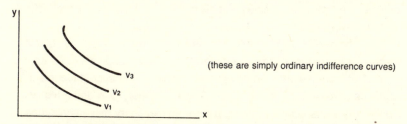

(these are simply ordinary indifference curves)

In this yx space vertical parallelism (V.P.) is defined to be V.P.yx→ $\partial v/\partial x = h_1(x)$, in which h_1 is some function. In the above graph this would mean that the tangent lines have identical slope, independent of v. Horizontal parallelism (H.P.) is the same notion in the horizontal direction. For the other spaces we would have V.P.vx→ $\partial v/\partial x = h_2(x)$ and V.P.vy→ $\partial v/\partial y = h_3(y)$.

The conditions under which cost-benefit analysis is consistent with the maximization of expected utility are, for all i, (1) V.P.yx$_i$, (2) V.P.vx$_i$, (3) H.P.vy, and (4) V.P.vy.

In applying cost-benefit analysis to the study of revolutions a modified conception of utility is also adopted. The maximization of expected-utility hypothesis is based on cardinal utility. This representation, however, is not assumed to reflect introspective satisfaction. (For a discussion of this point, see William J. Baumol, "The Cardinal Utility Which Is Ordinal," *The Economic Journal*, LXVIII:272 (December, 1958), pp. 665–72.) In Olson's analysis and its extension by other scholars, we must assume that the utility indices do reflect an individual's degree of satisfaction.

assumed is that people behave in a manner consistent with the maximization of expected utility hypothesis. In other words, it is assumed that men act *as if* they were maximizing their expected utility.[12] The actual process by which they arrive at the decisions that govern their behavior is unlikely to resemble the above account. For our purposes, we need not consider why men behave rationally, assuming that the do. However, if we are to base a theory of revolutions on the assumption that men *behave* rationally, it is probably worthwhile to investigate this assumption.

Unfortunately, it is exceedingly difficult to determine whether men behave in a rational manner, in the sense in which the term is being used here. We cannot independently assess both an individual's beliefs regarding the probability that an event will occur and the value he places on the outcome, should that event occur. Empirical tests of rationality are often based on some rather dubious additional assumptions, such as the assumption that utility is a linear function of money.[13] Given the problems involved in testing, we would hardly want to accept the results of these tests as conclusive evidence. However, if we are willing to lend any credence at all to the testing procedures, it appears that people do not, in fact, always behave rationally.

This result poses problems. The discussion of Olson's theory presented above assumed that the individual who had to decide whether or not he should participate in a revolutionary movement would act rationally. If the individual does not act in this way, there is no reason why the conclusions of Olson's theory should hold. In other words, the assumption of rational behavior is needed to explain why collective action should occur only under certain types of conditions, namely, when selective incentives are provided or when the individual believes that his actions will have a noticeable effect on the provision of the good sought by collective action.

At this point one could simply dismiss Olson's results (as an empirical theory) on the grounds that they depend on a false assumption. Given the state of political research on revolutions, I believe that such a judgment would be unreasonably harsh. If an alternative theory provided a highly satisfactory explanation of participation in revolutionary movements, one

---

[12]The general notion is that if an outside observer knew the relevant beliefs and valuations of a certain individual, he could calculate that individual's optimal course of action. It is assumed that this course of action would be the one chosen by the individual.

[13]Some of the tests of economically rational behavior are discussed in Donald Davidson and Patrick Suppes, in collaboration with Sidney Siegel, *Decision Making: An Experimental Approach* (Stanford: Stanford University Press, 1957); J. Marschak, "Decision Making: Economic Aspects," *International Encyclopedia of the Social Sciences,* 4 (1968), pp. 42–55; Lynne Ofshe and Richard Ofshe, *Utility and Choice in Social Interaction* (N.J.: Prentice-Hall, 1970); and John Wise and Pan A. Yotopoulos, "The Empirical Content of Rationality: A Test for a Less Developed Economy," *Journal of Political Economy,* 77 (1969), pp. 976–1004.

might legitimately demand a great deal of any competitive theory. But no such alternative theory is available. Under these circumstances, it is perhaps wise to practice toleration.

Nevertheless, if empirical studies are not to be totally disregarded, some modification of the maximization of expected utility hypothesis is required. The easiest way to do this is to assume that although people do not always act rationally, they generally do so in some types of situations, including the ones under consideration.[14] At present, empirical studies indicate only that we do not know under what conditions people act rationally. We do not even know whether some types of people generally act rationally while others do not or whether any individual's propensity to behave rationally depends on his perception of the type of choice situation he is in. Thus, we have no evidence that the above assumption is false; of course, we also have no evidence that it is true.

If this solution is deemed "too" *ad hoc* (which it is), Olson's theory could be interpreted as being applicable only to those individuals who behave in a manner consistent with the maximization of expected utility hypothesis This poses some problems of testability of the theory. These, however, are not of immediate concern. For the present, it is sufficient to note that although the theory on this intepretation is not strictly empirical in that it does not tell us the conditions under which people will participate in revolutionary movements, it may nevertheless be of considerable importance for an analysis of revolutions since, if the argument is correct, the common notion that rational individuals who sincerely desire a revolution will act so as to bring that revolution about may be invalid.

Revolutionary Participation: The Dilemma of the Rational Man

Let us consider now the situation of the individual who sympathizes with the revolutionaries. He may favor the revolution because he believes that his

---

[14]This is similar to the view set forth by Milton Friedman in "The Methodology of Positive Economics," in *Readings in the Philosophy of the Social Sciences,* ed. by May Brodbeck (New York: Macmillan, 1968), pp. 508–28. Despite this similarity, no instrumentalist overtones are intended. In particular, I do not agree with the view that the truth of the rationality assumption is unimportant. I do agree with the views of Paul Samuelson in "Comment on Ernest Nagel's 'Assumptions in Economic Theory,' " in *The Collected Scientific Papers of Paul A. Samuelson,* vol. 2, ed. by Joseph Stiglitz (Cambridge: MIT Press, 1966), pp. 1772–78, regarding the desirability of correcting inaccurate assumptions. However, our concern here does not primarily lie with theories of choice behavior but with theories of revolution. Several attempts have been made at constructing more realistic theories of rationality. At present, however, these theories are very difficult to work with.

personal position would be improved under the revolutionary regime or because he feels that other people would be better off in a revolutionary society. The reasons why any individual wants a revolution are not treated within the rational-choice context. These are only mentioned to emphasize again that the postulated self-interested individual need not be completely selfish.

For the present, we will discuss the case where there is only one revolutionary movement (which may or may not consist of a coalition of different groups). This case has been analyzed by Ireland, Silver and Tullock.[15] Although the analysis here is slightly different, the basic results are the same and are in accord with Olson's comments on decision making in cases in which the "quantity" of the public good is fixed and the outcome of any action is unknown.

The potential revolutionary in this situation must choose between two feasible courses of action: he can actively participate in the revolutionary movement, or he can stay at home, "wishing them well." If this individual does not believe that his participation will have any noticeable impact on the likelihood that the revolution will occur, and if he does not expect to receive special rewards for participation, the expected utility of his alternative courses of action may be represented as follows[16]:

$$E(P) = pR - E(C)$$
$$E(I) = pR$$

where P refers to participation, I to inaction, p to the probability that the revolution will succeed, R to the value the individual attaches to living in a revolutionary society as opposed to the status quo, and E(C) to the costs the individual expects to bear if he participates in the movement. These costs include such things as the possibility of being killed, wounded, or imprisoned, the possibility of suffering severe sanctions should the revolution fail, and the costs the revolutionary suffers from "foregone opportunities" (such as having a secure and comfortable position under the status quo).

The rational individual in this choice situation will obviously remain inac-

[15]Thomas Ireland, "The Rationale of Revolt," *Papers on Non-Market Decision Making,* 3 (1967), pp. 49–66; Morris Silver, "Political Revolution and Repression: An Economic Approach," *Public Choice,* XVII (Spring, 1974), pp. 63–71; and Gordon Tullock, "The Paradox of Revolution," *Public Choice,* XI (Fall, 1971), pp. 89–99.

[16]This is assuming that the individual has no desire to change the nature of the revolutionary movement. If he does, and if his valuation of the nature of the movement is independent of his valuation of the occurrence of the revolution, we may simply add in an expression referring to the

tive, since both courses of action yield the same expected benefits and the expected costs are higher if he participates. This, of course, assumes that the individual places some value on his life and liberty, both of which will be threatened to some extent if he joins a revolutionary movement.

Under the simple model used here, the individual becomes a "free rider"—that is, he anticipates no additional benefits from participation, adopting a "let Joe do it" stance. Of course, if everyone else follows suit, no one will participate, and the revolution will not occur. The implications are somewhat strange. It is perfectly possible for an individual's expected utility for participation to be positive and greater than the individual's valuation of remaining in the status quo. If everyone in this situation becomes a free rider, the resulting outcome will be a continuation of the status quo. However, these individuals could have attained a more preferred outcome had they all participated in the revolutionary movement. In other words, it is possible under the model used here for rational individuals to wind up in a worse position than a group of irrational individuals with the same preferences.[17]

Unfortunately, under the conception of rationality used here, the individual can recognize this dilemma and still have no incentive to modify his behavior, unless he believes that other people will react to his nonparticipation. If he assumes, as is probable in large groups, that other people will not base their decision to participate on his actions, then unless he expects his own actions to significantly affect the chances of a revolution occurring, he will be better off if he does not participate, whether or not the other people do.

Of course, the model used here is not applicable in all situations. Some individuals may expect to receive certain "selective incentives" or private benefits that affect their decisions. These incentives may be of two forms: coercion or private benefits from participation. Coercion refers to the use or threat of sanctions should the individual refuse to participate. The use of this type of incentive introduces a cost to inaction and may amount to providing some measure of excludability in the consumption of the public good. The private benefits that an individual may receive include such things as expectations of high office or other material rewards, should the revolution suc-

---

nature of the movement. Basically, so long as the individual does not expect to have any significant impact, the same conclusion holds. If the likelihood that the nature of the movement remains the same whether or not the individual participates, the individual should not participate.

The model as formulated here also neglects the possibility of the outcome being a stalemate situation and assumes that the individual's valuation of a revolutionary outcome does not depend on the number of people who participated in the struggle.

[17]Olson, pp. 9–10, compares this to the situation of firms in a competitive market, in which all firms would benefit if prices rose, but it is to each firm's advantage not to restrict the supply of the good it provides.

ceed. They may also include any psychological gratification the individual receives only if he participates.[18]

Incorporating selective incentives in the above equations yields

$$E(P) = pR + E(M) + G - E(C)$$

$$E(I) = pR - E(S)$$

where E(M) refers to the expected private benefits of a "material" nature, G is the gains of a "psychological" nature directly obtainable through participation, and E(S) is the expected value of the sanctions that the individual may suffer if he remains inactive. Clearly, all selective incentives must be "large enough" to make the individual better off if he participates. Theoretically, there is no reason to separate psychological and material benefits as was done here. In fact, there probably is no completely satisfactory way to separate these factors. Nevertheless, in many cases one can distinguish between the two, and since it will be necessary to make this distinction when empirical evidence is considered, it is convenient to introduce the distinction at this stage.

There is only a limited range of material benefits that are likely to serve as inducements to revolutionary action. The expectation of high political office, should the revolution succeed, is an obvious benefit of this type. This benefit, however, is relevant only to the leaders of revolutionary movements. After all, there are relatively few high political offices in any society, and it is not likely that the average potential revolutionary would believe that he had any significant chance of getting one of these. For the average person, the rewards of looting or possible preferential treatment in the aftermath of a revolution are more likely sources of material benefit. Even if no such benefits are available, however, the average person might still be induced to participate in revolutionary action by perceived psychological benefits of participation or by the threatened or actual use of coercion against nonparticipants.

Finally, we must modify the above equations to take into account the

---

[18]Tullock, "The Paradox of Revolution," uses an "entertainment value of participation" in the equations he develops and suggests that it is unlikely to be important. This factor is presumably equivalent to the psychological benefits used here. I think that Tullock's characterization of "entertainment," however, is quite misleading. There are a variety of psychological benefits other than sheer "entertainment." An individual may dislike the idea of being a "free rider" and derive satisfaction from the belief that he is "doing his share." In Marxist analysis, furthermore, there is the suggestion that workers can achieve their freedom through revolutionary struggle. Anyone who believes this and values his freedom might obtain considerable satisfaction from revolutionary participation. In short, although I would agree with Tullock that entertainment per se is probably not an important factor, I am not at all sure that other psychological benefits can be so easily dismissed.

possibility that individual action is believed to significantly alter the chances that the revolution will occur.[19] The resulting equations become:

$$E(P) = p_1 R + E(M) + G - E(C)$$

$$E(I) = p_2 R - E(S)$$

where p_1 and p_2 are the respective probabilities that the revolution will occur.

Under these conditions, a rational individual may participate in a revolutionary movement even if no selective incentives are available, provided that p_1 is sufficiently greater than p_2. Generally speaking, however, this type of consideration is likely to be relevant to only three types of people, all of whom probably constitute a rather small force numerically. The first type includes all people who believe that their individual contribution will be very great. These people are probably the ones generally designated as the revolutionary leaders.

The second type of person who might participate due to the effect his actions might have on the chances for the success of the revolution is what is commonly termed a "fanatic." This person places such a high value on the success of the movement relative to the costs of participation that even the most minute increase in the probability of success more than compensates him for the expected costs of participation. If the theory is to have any empirical relevance, we must follow Olson and assume that this type of individual is very rare.

Finally, the "average" individual, who is neither a fanatic nor a revolutionary genius, might participate if the situation is viewed as being extremely close so that even a small contribution to the revolutionary effort might have a significant impact on the chances of victory. This situation will probably also be empirically trivial. If no selective incentives are provided, the only people who should participate at the outset are the leaders and the fanatics. These, acting alone, will probably not be able to bring the revolution very close to success. Even if they can, however, the average nonparticipant might well decide that since these people are obviously "excellent" revolutionaries, they will be able to complete the job without outside assistance and that, at any rate, his contribution would not make much difference.

---

[19]This is basically a modified form of Olson's "size principle." The actual "size principle" derived by Olson will not be considered since it assumes (a) decision making under certainty and (b) that the public good takes the form of a direct monetary payment to the individual. (This latter assumption need not be made if we are willing to postulate a cardinal and interpersonally comparable index of utility.) Neither assumption is used here. This discussion, however, does seem to be in accord with Olson's general remarks concerning situations in which an individual's actions are believed to have a noticeable effect on the supply of the good or the distribution of the costs and benefits to others in a group.

In summary, the theory relies on two factors to explain participation: selective incentives and the possibility that an individual's actions will have a noticeable impact on the chances of revolutionary success. Both factors may be used to explain the participation of revolutionary leaders.[20] The participation of the masses, however, must largely be explained by three types of selective incentives: coercion, psychological gratification, and direct or anticipated material rewards.

Revolutionary Participation:
The Element of Uncertainty

So far the analysis has been based on the assumption that it is possible to estimate all of the relevant probabilities. This assumption may be overly restrictive. One might argue that although in a given situation it may be possible to estimate the probabilities of revolution, *given* the number of revolutionaries, there seems to be no way of directly estimating the probability that other people will participate and that there is no reason to expect anyone to act as though this feat could be performed. In short, one might claim that the type of choice situation assumed in the above analysis is inappropriate and that the situation should be analyzed as a problem of decision-making under uncertainty (i.e., decision-making in which certain relevant probabilities cannot be estimated).

If the choice situation is viewed in these terms, the only feasible way to analyze the problem of collective action is to rely on game theory. This type of analysis is quite complex. For our purposes, there is little reason to go into various ramifications of game theory since, at the present time, game theorists have not developed any commonly accepted solution to the type of problem under consideration. Instead of analyzing the problem of collective action under uncertainty in any depth, then, the analysis will be restricted to a simplified discussion of some of the basic issues.

We will consider the situation of an individual who is sympathetic to the revolution. He does not know what the other people in the society will do but can estimate what will happen *if* such-and-such percentage participates. This individual expects that his actions will have no significant impact on the probability of revolution and does not expect to receive any selective incentives. We assume that the individual believes there are some costs to participation. In this case, he prefers a situation in which everyone else (or a

---

[20]For a more detailed analysis of the role of leaders, see Norman Frohlich, Joe A. Oppenheimer, and Oran R. Young, *Political Leadership and Collective Goods* (Princeton: Princeton University Press, 1971).

sizable percentage of the others) participates while he does not to a situation in which everyone, including himself, participates. If the individual strongly dislikes the status quo, he may prefer participating with the other people to a situation in which no one participates and the status quo remains. However, assuming that his actions do not have a noticeable impact, his least favored alternative will occur if he participates and no one else joins him.

This type of situation may be depicted by the "payoff" vectors of all people who want a revolution. For simplicity, however, we will consider only the alternatives available to one individual as he evaluates the situation in relation to the actions of other people who might or might not participate. Given the above preferences, the payoffs to the individual may be represented in the following way[21]:

		Others	
		participation	nonparticipation
Individual	participation	.8	0
	nonparticipation	1	.2

The numbers here are only intended to reflect the individual's preference for the various possible outcomes.

In this situation, Olson's conclusions are quite evident: whether others participate or not, the individual in question is better off if he does not participate.[22] He should, then, try to become a free rider.

If the individual does expect to receive selective incentives, or if he expects to significantly affect the course of the revolution, the relative value of the possible outcomes may change. For example, some leaders may be in the following situation:

		Others	
		participation	nonparticipation
Individual	participation	1	.2
	nonparticipation	.8	0

---

[21]A similar representation of Olson's theory may be found in Russel Hardin, "Collective Action as an Agreeable n-Prisoners' Dilemma," *Behavioral Science,* 16:5 (September, 1971), pp. 472–81. For a more general treatment, see Robert Axelrod, *Conflict of Interest* (Chicago: Markham, 1970).

[22]Note that on an n-dimensional representation, the structure of the payoffs would yield an instance of the notorious "Prisoner's Dilemma" game. In this situation, a group of irrational players might each do better than a group of rational players since the equilibrium solution for rational players is not Pareto optimal.

This might occur if the leader felt his actions alone could provide considerable impetus toward the formation of a revolutionary movement and his actions, in conjunction with those of others, would significantly increase the probability of revolutionary success. In this case, the rational individual would participate since, no matter what the others do, he gains by participation. Conceivably, even people who are not leaders may be in a similar situation if the value they place on the selective incentives is sufficiently high.

Of course, in some cases the choice situation may not be clear-cut. The individual might believe that he alone could not start a revolutionary movement, so that if others do not participate, he would be better off if he did not participate. However, if a revolutionary movement had been formed, the individual might feel that his actions would significantly affect revolutionary fortunes to an extent great enough to offset the costs of participation. This situation might be represented by the following payoff structure:

		Others	
		participation	nonparticipation
Individual	participation	1	0
	nonparticipation	.8	.2

Without going into the complexities of n-person game theory, there is no way to analyze this situation. Intuitively, however, we would expect that the individual's course of action would be heavily dependent on the actions of the other people. If others are in a similar situation, their actions may also be mutually interdependent. If this is the case, the outcome at any particular point may be indeterminate.[23]

The use of game theory (at least in this simplified form) yields substantially the same conclusions as the use of cost-benefit analysis. If there are no selective incentives, and the individual expects to have no noticeable impact, he should not participate, whether or not he is willing to estimate the proba-

---

[23]The type of indeterminacy in this model is somewhat analogous to the indeterminacy of Olson's "intermediate group," in which an individual's actions have a noticeable impact but no individual has an incentive to provide the public good by himself. However, Olson's major concern in this area seems to lie with the possibility that individuals in small groups might engage in strategic interaction, and it will thus not be possible to estimate the probability that the good will be provided if any individual fails to participate.

The remaining possible permutation of payoffs is likely to arise if the group is "privileged," that is, if one individual would benefit even if he paid the entire cost of the good, although he would naturally prefer others to share the burden of its provision. Since this situation is of no practical importance for the study of revolutions, it will not be discussed here.

ble actions of others. If the above factors are present, however, the individual may be in a situation in which participation is rational.

Despite the similarity of the conclusions reached by these two modes of analysis, the use of game theory to analyze revolutionary action offers one advantage over the more traditional cost-benefit calculations. In game theory, the dilemma of the rational man in certain types of choice situations becomes painfully apparent since it is clear that a group of people who are individually rational may be collectively "irrational" in terms of achieving a common goal. It is probably for this reason that game theorists are far more concerned about this problem than those who use the more traditional form of analysis in public goods theory.[24] The concern of the game theorists seems to be quite justified, as experimental evidence, at least on two-person games, indicates that people in this type of situation often do not behave in the predicted fashion. Perhaps ultimately the work of game theorists in this area will prove to be of great importance to the study of collective action. At present, however, the basic dilemma posed by the games theory analogue to the free-rider problem has eluded satisfactory solution. For this reason, I will base the remainder of the discussion on the earlier type of cost-benefit analysis.

Revolutionary Participation: Competition Among Revolutionary Groups

Although coalitions among revolutionary movements are quite common, it is often the case that at any given time, there are two or more revolutionary groups that are not cooperating with each other.[25] The inclusion of more than one revolutionary movement does not change the above conclusions. However, since this situation does not seem to have been considered in applications of Olson's theory, and since it is empirically relevant, a brief discussion is included here.

We will consider the choice situation presented when there are a number, say n, of competing revolutionary movements. Ignoring the possibility of stalemate,[26] there are now n+1 possible outcomes: Each of the n rev-

---

[24]For a discussion of the basic problem, see Anatol Rapoport and Albert Chammah, *Prisoner's Dilemma* (Ann Arbor: University of Michigan Press, 1965). For a discussion of some of the proposed solutions, see Hardin, "Collective Action"; R. Duncan Luce and Howard Raiffa, *Games and Decisions* (New York: Wiley, 1957), pp. 94–102; and Martin Shubik, "Game Theory, Behavior, and the Paradox of the Prisoner's Dilemma: Three Solutions," *The Journal of Conflict Resolution,* XIV:2 (June, 1970), pp. 181–93.
[25]This is always the case if we include the possibility of an individual forming his own movement.
[26]Including the possibility of stalemates only complicates the analysis without altering conclusions. For a discussion of the basic model (applied to voting) that explicity includes a consideration of

olutionary movements could win, or the government could win. An individual's expected utility of inaction will, in the absence of selective incentives, be:

$$E(I) = \sum_{i=1}^{n+1} p_i^0 R_i$$

where p_i^0 refers to the probability that the ith group will win if the individual does not participate, and R_i refers to the individual's utility for the outcome characterized by the success of the ith group. (For notational convenience, R_{n+1} is taken to refer to government victory.)

The individual's expected utility of participating in any revolutionary movement, say the kth, is, similarly,

$$E(P^k) = \sum_{i=1}^{n+1} p_i^k R_i - E(C_k)$$

where $E(C_k)$ refers to the expected costs of participating in the kth group, and p_i^k refers to the probability that the ith group will be successful if the individual joins the kth movement.

As before, we assume that the individual chooses the course of action that yields the highest net gain.[27] In particular, he will only participate in any movement if his expected utility of participating in that movement exceeds his expected utility of remaining inactive. Assuming that there are some costs to participation, this means that the individual who expects to have only a negligible impact in any movement, so that $p_i^0 = p_i^k$ for all i and k, should stay at home.

The basic conclusions of Olson's analysis retain their full force even if there is competition among revolutionary movements. In fact, within the general rational-choice framework, Olson's conclusions hold for all of the definitions of an individual's choice situation considered here, with the possible exception of some situations in decision making under uncertainty. Even in this latter case, the general analysis supports Olson's conclusions. The

stalemates, see Richard D. McKelvey and Peter C. Ordeshook, "A General Theory of the Calculus of Voting," in *Mathematical Applications in Political Science,* VI, ed. by James F. Herndon and Joseph L. Bernd (Charlottesville: University Press of Virginia, 1972), pp. 32–78. Many of the conclusions of these authors, however, do not apply to revolutionary situations since the outcome of a revolutionary struggle, unlike that of an electoral contest, is subject to no known decision rule.

[27] This implies that if an individual participates at all, he need not participate in support of the group he most favors.

only reason for isting this case as a possible exception is that game theorists have developed other solution conceptions that, if adopted, would run counter to these conclusions.

Revolutionary Participation: Empirical Evidence

Olson's theory and its extension by the other authors discussed above seem to make a good deal of sense. If we are willing to accept the concept of rationality on which it is based, there seems to be little way to avoid the conclusion that the public good aspect of revolutions should not motivate people to participate in the revolution. Furthermore, the general treatment of collective action is somewhat appealing in that it explains a wide variety of political behavior in a simple manner. And the explanation does indicate the conditions under which collective action should occur and the reasons why these factors are relevant. In short, the theory, if confirmed, would be an extremely significant contribution to political science. But theories, however neat and psychologically appealing, must also pass tests of empirical adequacy. We are, after all, using our theories to explain empirical phenomena, and if these theories are disconfirmed by events in the real world, some modification must be made. In particular, if this theory is to provide us with a satisfactory explanation of revolutionary participation, it must be able to account for the nature of participation in actual revolutions.

It is, however, difficult to determine the empirical adequacy of this particular theory, since all the relevant factors are purely subjective. We have no way of knowing an individual's subjective estimation of the extent to which his actions will alter the probability of revolutionary success. Nor do we have any independent assessment of the utility of individuals for particular benefits or costs. In short, the theory as stated cannot be tested. To subject it to empirical investigation, a variety of additional assumptions must be made. The discussion here will follow what I take to be the general procedure used by Olson in evaluating the evidence he uses for his theory.[28]

It will be assumed, in the first place, that people in revolutionary situations act rationally. This assumption is necessary since none of the above conclusions need apply to irrational individuals. We will also assume that the number of fanatics in any society is very small, so that an individual's participation cannot, except in rare cases, be explained in terms of the minute increase in the probability of success that he might attribute to his actions. It

---

[28]See, in particular, Olson, pp. 45n, 48n, 61n, 160n, 161n.

is further assumed that an individual's estimate of the differences in probability attributable to his actions is "reasonable," that is, that with the exception of some of the great revolutionary leaders, the individual does not expect his actions to have any great impact on the course of the revolution. Similarly, an individual's expectation of receiving material benefits is assumed to be "reasonable." In particular, I assume that the average person anticipates no material benefits, other than those obtained through looting or promised by leaders. Finally—and this is crucial—we must assume that psychological benefits provide negligible selective incentives.

Under these conditions, the average individual would only participate if he were either coerced or received a direct or promised payment for participation. Leaders, on the other hand, might participate since they might expect to receive other selective incentives, such as high office should the revolution succeed, and since their actions might reasonably be expected to significantly affect the chances of revolutionary success. Unless there is widespread looting or evidence that large numbers of people have been bribed, or unless coercion is widespread, then, there should be no mass revolution.[29]

The problem of defining "revolution" in this context is not particularly troublesome. The theory is designed to hold in all instances of collective action, that is, action that is expected to further the common interests of a group of people. If an event is included that might, more appropriately, be termed a rebellion rather than a revolution, the result is not disastrous since presumably the theory should hold for that event as well.

What is slightly more troublesome is to determine how many people constitute a "large number" and what kind of actions fall under the category of revolutionary participation. In terms of the number of participants, the theory itself is not precise, and there is little point in introducing an artificial precision. However, since there should be relatively few leaders and fanatics, it seems reasonable to suppose that if the number of participants exceeds a few hundred, the extent of participation cannot be explained by postulating that all of the participants were of these two types.

In considering acts of revolutionary participation, more discretion must be used. Most people use the term to refer to such things as riots, demonstrations, and other illegal acts against property rights or people representing the status quo. For our purposes, however, care must be taken to exclude those acts, such as land seizures, that result in a direct private gain to the participating individuals, since such acts could obviously be explained in terms of the selective incentives available.

---

[29]This conclusion is explicit in Ireland, "The Rationale of Revolt," p. 60, and implicit in Olson, p. 106.

Let us consider whether the theory of rational participation seems reasonable in light of the events that occurred during two revolutions: the French and the Russian. These revolutions are chosen because they are classic examples; virtually every author, no matter how he defines "revolution," includes these cases as two of the great revolutions. The discussion here in no way presupposes to be an analysis of the participation in these revolutions. It is intended only to provide an account of the nature of participation that is sufficient to allow us to decide if the events that took place are in accord with the type of participation predicted by the rational-participation theory.

The French Revolution of 1789 seems, by all accounts, to have been a mass revolution. Indeed, in searching through historical accounts, it is difficult to find reference to any group of people who were not, in one way or another, engaged in revolutionary activities. If any action can be said to have "sparked" the revolution, it is probably the demand of the French noblemen for a greater share in the control of government and the reconvention of the Estates-General. Even at the outset, however, the struggle was by no means limited to that between the king and the nobility. Delegates from the Third Estate, representing, by and large, the bourgeoisie, immediately demanded greater representation. One might, of course, argue that these men were the leaders of their class and that their actions could consequently be explained in terms of the rational-participation theory.

It would be difficult, however, to explain similarly the actions of the lower classes. Even before the convocation of the Estates-General, the dissatisfaction of the workers and peasants had manifested itself in a series of riots, demonstrations, and illegal strikes. Peasants refused to pay manorial dues. Workers demanded everything from more food to a new political order. In July, following the dismissal of Jacques Necker, the popular minister, and the concentration of royalist troops about Versailles, thousands of Parisians began a series of demonstrations that culminated in the famous storming of the Bastille. It is doubtful that the people engaging in these actions had any hopes of winning a high political office or securing other material benefits. Nor is there evidence that these people were coerced into risking their lives. And, it is hardly reasonable to suppose that one demonstrator, more or less, would have significantly affected the course of events.

The extent of popular participation during this period is, I believe, sufficient to challenge the empirical adequacy of the rational-participation theory. Mass participation in this revolution, however, was by no means ended with the storming of the Bastille. During the Great Fear that spread through the countryside in late July, peasants burned manor houses and destroyed feudal records. In towns throughout the nation the old authorities were overthrown and replaced by new governmental bodies. These popular rebellions, it should be noted, were by no means "costless." Many of the revolutionaries who stormed the Bastille were killed. Later rebellions fared no better. The bourgeois leaders at the helm of the Assembly were not at all favorably disposed toward "mob rule" and imposed severe sanctions, including the death penalty, for rebellion.

The list of mass-participation events in the French Revolution could go on almost indefinitely. Some of these events were of great significance in the Revolution. The storming of the Tuileries in 1792 led to the execution of Louis XVI and initiated what has been termed the "second" French Revolution. The Parisian crowds that invaded the National Convention halls in 1793 and arrested Girondist deputies secured the victory of the radical Mountain wing of the Jacobins, headed by Robespierre, over its more conservative opponents. Nor was popular participation limited to the radical side. The peasant revolt in the Vendée, which flared up in 1793 and lasted until 1796, was decidedly counterrevolutionary, as, of course, were the actions of the refractory priests. All in all, it would be very difficult to deny the mass character of this revolution.

The French Revolution is not a lone exception. In analyzing the Russian Revolution, we also find a degree of participation that exceeds the explanatory capacities of the rational participation theory. There was certainly a widespread mass movement in the abortive revolution of 1905. Following the demonstration on "Bloody Sunday," when a crowd of peaceful petitioners was dispersed in a most brutal fashion, labor unrest spread throughout the country. One source estimates that about one and a half million workers participated in political strikes in the course of the year, an extraordinary figure considering that at this time there were only about two million industrial workers in the country.[30] The general strike that broke out in October was so widespread that it virtually paralyzed the entire nation. In several cases, the strikes developed into armed uprisings that, although ultimately unsuccessful, did, nevertheless, receive widespread support.

The fall of the Romanov dynasty in 1917 was also largely the result of an unorganized and spontaneous popular uprising. On March 8, crowds of women in Petrograd began a demonstration that was to initiate a series of strikes in the city that, by the third day, encompassed an estimated 200,000 workers. At first, the crowd, armed with sticks and stones, clashed with police and troops brought in to suppress the rebellion. The situation seemed much like a repeat performance of what had happened in 1905. This time, however, the soldiers mutinied and joined the revolutionaries. Within a week

---

[30]William Henry Chamberlin, *The Russian Revolution*, vol. 1 (New York: Grosset & Dunlap, 1965), p. 63. Note also that unions at this time were not legal.

the revolution had spread to Moscow and the rest of the country. The Tsar was forced to abdicate and power passed to the Duma and the Soviets.

The revolution, of course, was not completed at this stage. But it was begun—and through the initiative of crowds of people that individually could not reasonably have expected to have a significant influence on the course of events. During subsequent months, popular participation remained quite high. For our purposes, however, there is no point in going over these events since the extent of participation during the March Revolution seems quite sufficient to counter the notion that the revolution was brought about by a small "elitist conspiracy."

Both the Russian and the French revolutions provide evidence against the rational-participation theory. One might, of course, aruge that it is not the theory that is faulty but the additional assumptions used to test it. In particular, the lack of consideration of possible psychological benefits seems highly questionable. The inclusion of these factors, however, makes it impossible to test the theory,[31] and I am not convinced of the value of accepting yet another untestable theory. Furthermore, if psychological factors are actually that important in explaining revolutionary participation, we need to know more about these factors, including the conditions under which they are likely to provide major incentives for large numbers of people. In short, I doubt the wisdom of trying to "save" the theory by relying on unspecified and unanalyzed "psychological benefits."

Conclusion

It is difficult to assess the overall contribution of the rational-choice theory of revolutionary participation. The explanation that the theory provides is certainly logically coherent and, to a certain extent, eminently plausible. It specifies factors that are relevant to revolutionary action and explains why these are relevant in terms of rational behavior. Furthermore, the theory makes considerable sense, especially in view of the rarity of mass revolutions. On the other hand, the fact that thousands (even millions) of people have engaged in revolutionary action shows that the theory either underemphasizes the importance of psychological factors or overemphasizes the extent of individual rationality in human behavior.

This result suggests two possible ways of developing rational-choice theories of revolutionary action. The first involves incorporating a more detailed account of the nature and effect of psychological factors into the

---

[31] This point is fully recognized by Olson, pp. 61n, 160n.

theory. Although this task is difficult, it may be facilitated by prior investigation of the conditions under which any psychological benefits are needed to explain participation in collective action. Olson suggests that these conditions are related to the goals of collective action. Specifically, he argues that the theory might not be useful for an analysis of organizations that have noneconomic objectives, both because psychological factors are likely to be more important in these groups and because people probably act less rationally in trying to secure noneconomic objectives.[32]

If further research indicates that Olson's hypothesis is correct, subsequent analysis might focus on the way in which participation is elicited in organizations with noneconomic objectives. Such research would have to be based on an interaction between theoretical and empirical considerations. Thus, from a preliminary empirical investigation of such organizations, it is possible to develop tentative hypotheses about the role and nature of psychological factors in explaining participation. These hypotheses may then be used to guide research about participation in other organizations of a similar nature. Such efforts may enable us to develop fairly refined hypotheses that will help explain how psychological factors affect participation in revolutionary movements, as well as other forms of collective action.

A second line of investigation could focus on the assumption of individual rationality that forms the basis of Olson's theory. This type of modification of the theory is far more radical than the previous one, since it involves a modification of the core assumptions of the theory. This means that it is likely to entail a more complex modification of the theory. Nevertheless, there is a considerable amount of work being done in the area of decision theory, and it ultimately may be possible to develop a theory of collective action that relies on a more realistic conception of human rationality than the usual maximization of expected-utility hypothesis. One aspect of this type of modification that seems particularly important for an analysis of revolutionary behavior concerns the effect of social conditions on the nature of collective action. People, after all, live in societies, and it is not unreasonable to suppose that their mode of behavior will be influenced by their social experiences.[33] Since revolutions often seem to involve changed modes of behavior on the part of large numbers of people, it is quite possible that this facet of the investigation may be of crucial importance in explaining participation in revolutionary movements.

---

[32]Olson, pp. 159–65.

[33]For a discussion of this that proceeds from a different perspective, see Otto Kirchheimer, "Private Man and Society," *Political Science Quarterly,* 81 (March, 1966), pp. 1–24. See also the discussion in Chapter 5, below, and the modifications of Olson introduced in Anthony Oberschall, *Social Conflict and Social Movements* (Englewood Cliffs, N.J.: Prentice-Hall, 1973).

As it stands, Olson's theory does not provide a wholly adequate explanation of individual participation in revolutionary movements. It seems likely that the problem with this theory stems from its relative neglect of psychological factors or from the conception of rationality on which the theory is based, or both. However, that the theory does not satisfy all the criteria required for adequate theories does not mean that it contributes nothing to the understanding of revolutions. As Barry has suggested, although there are many cases in which the level of participation exceeds the explanatory capacities of the rational-participation theory, it is probable that the conditions outlined by the theory are relevant to collective action.[34] In other words, although the extent of participation in revolutions and other forms of collective action cannot be fully explained in terms of selective incentives, it is likely that the presence or absence of these incentives does affect the level of participation. If this is the case (and an investigation of this should be feasible), then the theory may surely be considered quite useful for its delineation of some of the factors affecting collective action. The most plausible conclusion seems to be that the theory explains some, although not all, of the reasons for participation in revolutionary movements.

[34]Brian Barry, *Sociologists, Economists, and Democracy* (London: Collier, 1970), pp. 40–46.

THE PSYCHOLOGICAL BASIS
OF revolutionary action

One of the problems of the rational-choice explanation of participation in revolutionary movements is its relative neglect of psychological factors. Although the theory allows for the possibility that these factors may enter into rational calculations, it does not specify the nature of such factors, nor does it give any indication of the conditions under which psychological factors will be of major importance for large numbers of people in a given society. This means, in effect, that in cases in which psychology is a crucial motivating force, the rational-choice explanation of revolutionary action breaks down. The inability of rational-choice theories to cope with psychological factors in any detailed fashion does not, of course, imply that such theories are useless or that their basic conception is wrong. Nevertheless, it does indicate that psychological theories should be examined as a possible supplement or alternative to rational-choice theories.

This chapter focuses on the social-psychological explanation of revolutionary action proposed by Ted Gurr.[1] This work has been widely acclaimed as an outstanding psychological theory of political violence. Well it might. Gurr integrates an enormous amount of the psychologically oriented literature on rebellion and revolution under the rubric of a single theory.[2] This, in itself, is no easy feat. Studies that, either explicitly or implicitly, are based on social-psychological assumptions form a very large part of the literature on revolutions and related manifestations of political violence. By pulling this literature—or a large part of it—together, Gurr shows how the multiple social and psychological factors that have been used to explain aspects of the revolutionary process can be united into a single coherent explanation of political rebellion.

Gurr does this by extending the basic frustration-aggression hypothesis developed in psychological studies into the political realm. In simplified form, this hypothesis states that people who are frustrated are more likely to respond more aggressively than they would had they not been frustrated. In effect, then, frustration increases the probability of aggression. Gurr argues that in the political realm, there is a similar relationship between relative deprivation—or deprivation with respect to socially conditioned expectations—and political violence. So, relative deprivation and political violence are the social analogues of frustration and aggression. Further-more, like the frustration-aggression relationship, the relationship between relative deprivation and political violence may be mediated by numerous other factors.

This theory, and the frustration-aggression hypothesis on which it is based, will be briefly reviewed in the following sections. Although this review does not cover all aspects of Gurr's theory, it is sufficient for our purposes. In terms of the criteria for explanations developed in Chapter I, the theory obviously satisfies the first requirement: It specifies variables relevant to revolutions (as well as other forms of political violence) and the ways in which these are related to revolutions. In fact, the theory is stated in precisely these terms. The first criterion, then, poses no problem of evaluation.

The other two requirements placed on explanations, namely, the theoreti-cal and empirical justification of the relevancy of variables included in the theory, pose more difficult problems. For this reason, attention will be fo-cused on issues raised in connection with these latter criteria. The problem

---

[1]Gurr, *Why Men Rebel.* Unless otherwise noted, all references to Gurr are to this work.
[2]The major exception to this is the psychoanalytic literature, which Gurr does not discuss. This omission, however, is quite reasonable, as psychoanalytic theories are based on concepts and assumptions that are entirely different from the ones used by Gurr and related authors. Since psychoanalytic and social-psychological theories do not share the same core assumptions, they are not, properly speaking, part of the same "paradigm" and cannot easily be integrated with one another.

with the theoretical justification of the relevancy of variables used to explain revolutions is particularly crucial. As I argued above, if this criterion is not met, there is no way of telling whether a theory is an explanation of a given phenomenon or merely a statement of a list of spurious correlates associated with it. Since Gurr is relying on the frustration-aggression hypothesis to supply a theoretical justification for the variables he proposes, this claim must be examined.

An examination of the theoretical basis provided by the frustration-aggression hypothesis is a multifaceted task. The first problem is that while the concepts of relative deprivation and political violence, on the one hand, and frustration and aggression, on the other, are somewhat similar to each other, they are neither identical sets of ideas nor can one be subsumed under the other. This means that we must examine the central concepts used by Gurr to determine if the extension of psychological concepts from the interpersonal context, for which they were designed to apply, to the much broader social and political context can be justified on either theoretical or empirical grounds. A second problem is that whereas the frustration-aggression hypothesis applies to individuals, most of Gurr's hypotheses are formulated for whole societies. This, too, may complicate the problem of using the frustration-aggression hypothesis as the theoretical basis of Gurr's theory. Once these issues have been clarified, it is possible to evaluate the grounds on which explanatory variables were selected to determine whether the theory meets the theoretical justification criterion.

Finally, the empirical adequacy of the theory must be considered. While the discussion here is based on evidence provided by Gurr, other evidence will be brought in if it serves to clarify a dubious issue. In this way, it will hopefully be possible to examine problems with the type of evidence used by Gurr as well as to formulate an overall impression of the support this evidence provides the theory without attempting the nearly impossible task of synthesizing all evidence that might be relevant to this theory.

The Theory of Political Violence:
An Overview

Gurr's theory focuses on two aspects of political violence: its magnitude and its forms. The magnitude of political violence is conceived as a unidimensional variable, that is, societies can presumably be ordered according to the amount of political violence exhibited. The forms of political violence, on the other hand, refer to particular types of manifestations of politi-.

52

cal violence and are not treated as unidimensional attributes. Following Rummel,[3] Gurr distinguishes among three dimensions or forms of political violence: turmoil, conspiracy, and internal war. "Turmoil" refers to such unorganized, popular violence as riots and localized rebellions. "Conspiracy" includes all highly organized political violence that occurs with limited participation, such as coups, mutinies, and smallscale guerrilla warfare. "Internal war" refers to organized political violence with widespread participation, including large-scale guerrilla warfare, civil wars, and revolutions.

The theory itself may be divided into four parts. The first three are concerned with the magnitude of political violence and deal with what Gurr terms the development, politicization, and "actualization" of discontent within a society; the fourth examines the causes of specific forms of political violence. Since variables used in this task are many, only the most important ones will be discussed. For a more complete list, the reader is referred to Gurr's "diagrammatic exposition," which has been reproduced in the Appendix.

The major factors affecting the development of discontent in a society, Gurr argues, are the intensity and scope of relative deprivation. Relative deprivation is probably the single most important concept in this theory. It refers to the "perceived discrepancy between men's value expectations and their value capabilities" or, in other words, to the gap between what people think they are entitled to receive and what they believe they are capable of attaining under the status quo.[4] The intensity of relative deprivation in a society is the average intensity of the relative deprivation experienced by individuals in the society. The scope of relative deprivation refers to the proportion of people in a society who experience fairly intense degrees of relative deprivation.[5]

This part of the theory is somewhat confusing. We are told that relative deprivation causes discontent and also that the intensity of relative deprivation is defined as the "sharpness of discontent or anger to which it gives rise."[6] Furthermore, the potential for collective violence—the scope and intensity of people's *dispositions* to engage in violent action—is said to be affected by both the intensity and scope of discontent and by the intensity and scope of relative deprivation.[7] It appears that there is either one variable too many in this analysis or that the intensity of the relative-deprivation

---

[3]Rudolph J. Rummel, "Dimensions of Conflict Behavior Within and Between Nations," *General Systems Yearbook,* 8 (1963), pp. 1–50, and "Dimensions of Conflict Behavior, 1946–59," *Journal of Conflict Resolution,* X:1 (March, 1966), pp. 65–73.
[4]Gurr, p. 13.
[5]Gurr, p. 83.
[6]Gurr, pp. 21, 29.
[7]Gurr, pp. 24, 319.

concept needs to be redefined. The latter task seems more consistent with Gurr's theory and will be adopted here. It will be supposed that there is some cardinal and interpersonally comparable scale reflecting the perceptions of individuals concerning the discrepancy between their value expectations and their value capabilities.[8] This scale is distinct from one that might be used to represent individual discontent, and the corresponding social averages of the two variables are also distinct variables.

The preceding interpretation is used only because Gurr seems to view discontent as something other than relative deprivation. The discontent variable is generally stressed as intervening between relative deprivation and the potential for political violence. Although Gurr does not discuss "discontent," it is apparently intended to refer to some mental-state "link" between relative deprivation and the potential for political violence. I believe the discontent variable might well be deleted. It contributes little to the theory beyond raising a host of unpleasant questions regarding the role of mental events as causes of behavior. In fact, Gurr himself, after stressing the importance of this variable, deletes it from his diagrams. (See Appendix.)

If discontent is deleted, the theory (to this point) might be summarized by saying that the potential for collective violence in a society is some positive or increasing monotonic function of the intensity and scope of relative deprivation in a society.[9] This hypothesis, like all others in the book, is probabilistic, and the function relating these variables is thought to have an error component. In other words, the hypothesis states that societies with higher intensities and scopes of relative deprivation are more *likely* to have higher potentials for collective violence than are societies with lower intensities and scopes of relative deprivation.

The second part of the theory focuses on what Gurr terms the politicization of discontent. Basically, the potential for political violence in a society—a concept that is similar to the potential for collective violence except that it refers to the potential for directing violence against specifically political

---

[8]Note that this assumption is stronger than the corresponding assumption needed for individual utility in the rational-choice theory since it requires interpersonal comparability as well as cardinality. The assumption that the scales can be meaningfully compared across individuals is necessary if we are to aggregate individual intensities of relative deprivation to form a societal measure of relative deprivation.

[9]The societal potential for collective violence is presumably the average of the individual dispositions to engage in collective violence. Although the potential for collective violence is treated as a single variable, it is defined as the scope and intensity of dispositions to violent action. What Gurr apparently has in mind is that some overall potential for collective violence variable is to be formed through a combination of the scope and intensity variables, although it is not clear how this feat is to be accomplished. It is also unclear why the intensity and scope variables should be combined in this case but treated as separate variables in the case of relative deprivation,

objects—is thought to be an increasing monotonic function of the potential for collective violence in a society. The idea seems to be that if other things are equal, societies with higher potentials for collective violence in general should have higher potentials for specifically political violence. All other things, of course, are not always equal, and Gurr posits a number of other factors that affect the potential for specifically political violence. Of primary importance are the scope and intensity of the justifications for political violence. These factors, in turn, are thought to be dependent on a number of other societal conditions, including the legitimacy of the regime, the success of previous efforts at political violence, and the efficacy with which the regime has been able to alleviate problems of relative deprivation in the past.

The intensity of the justifications for political violence is a rather vague concept. Instead of defining this variable, Gurr takes it to be "a function first of the *range of circumstances* to which actual or threatened violence is thought to be an appropriate response, and second of the *relative desirability* of violence, in normative or utilitarian terms, vis-à-vis other responses."[10] It is difficult to see how these two components are to be combined into a single measure. Furthermore, the range component is itself unclear: there seems to be no way of either adequately classifying various possible types of circumstances or weighting these in importance to determine the proportion of possible circumstances to which violence would be considered an appropriate response. It is true, of course, that we do have some vague idea of what is meant by this term. But in this case—as well as in others—Gurr's definition does not go beyond this vague conception.

The third part of the theory deals with the actual magnitude of political violence in a society. This magnitude is thought to be dependent on three variables: the potential for political violence, the balance of regime to dissident coercive control, and the balance of regime to dissident institutional support. As with previous variables, the magnitude of political violence is taken as an increasing monotonic function of the potential for political violence. The type of functional dependence posited for the other two variables, however, is different: both the balance of coercive control and the balance of institutional support variables are thought to have curvilinear relationships with the magnitude of political violence. In other words, it is thought that as the ratio of dissident to regime coercive control (institutional support) increases to the point of equality, the magnitude of political violence is likely to similarly increase. Beyond the point of equality, however, an increase in this

---

[10]Gurr, p. 157.

ratio is thought to be accompanied by a decrease in the magnitude of political violence.

The final part of the theory concerns the determinants of the form of political violence, that is, the conditions under which the likely type of political violence exhibited will be internal war, turmoil, or conspiracy. According to Gurr, the factors that cause the different forms of political violence are "not different from those that determine the magnitude of political violence, but rather are combinations of particular levels or degrees of those variables."[11]

The first determinant of the forms of political violence concerns the types of people who suffer from severe relative deprivation. If relative deprivation affects both the elite and the masses, internal war is presumed as the likely outcome. Conspiracies are likely to occur when the elite alone suffers from relative deprivation, while mass relative deprivation by itself is thought to result in turmoil. A second major determinant is the ratio of dissident to regime coercive control. Internal war is posited as the most likely form of violence when this ratio approaches one—that is, when the coercive forces of both sides are approximately equal. When the regime maintains high coercive control, either turmoil or conspiracy occurs as the possible outcome. If regime control is very low, however, conspiracies are taken as the most likely form of political violence. Finally, the nature of institutional (or noncoerced) support is considered a relevant factor. Internal wars are again most likely to occur when the dissidents and the regime are equal in this respect. If dissidents have a rather low degree but wide scope of support, widespread turmoil is likely. However, if dissidents enjoy support that is relatively intense (that is, high in degree) but low in scope, conspiracy is thought to be the most likely outcome.[12]

The above outline is quite sketchy and by no means includes all of the variables Gurr uses in explaining political violence. But the major variables and the relationships among these have been outlined, and this should serve as a sufficient basis for a more general discussion of the theory and the problems it presents. It should be emphasized at this point that Gurr's theory does not tell us "why men rebel"; rather, it is an attempt to explain why *societies* have rebellions. All variables used in the study are attributes of societies, although they are often formed by taking the average value of the corresponding individual attributes. This point is important because, as I will try to show later, the attempt to base a theory about the behavior of groups of people or societies on individualist, psychological theory creates a variety of problems that are both severe and very difficult to overcome.

---

[11]Gurr, p. 334.
[12]Gurr, pp. 237, 280–81, 341–42.

The Psychological Basis: Frustration-Aggression Hypotheses

The frustration-aggression hypothesis, Gurr claims, provides the psychological mechanism underlying his theory of political violence.[13] This hypothesis, in several variants, has been popular among psychologists for a long time.[14] It states, basically, that the presence of a frustrating stimulus increases the likelihood that the frustrated organism will respond aggressively.[15] The hypothesis may be formulated in a completely probabilistic manner.[16] Frustration does not always lead to aggression; the frustrated person may become apathetic—or develop new goals. Nor does aggression always occur in response to frustration; people may imitate aggression or carry out aggressive acts on the command of an authority figure, even when there is no evidence of prior frustration. Frustration, however, is thought to be relevant to aggression in that it increases the probability of aggression.

Although definitions vary from author to author, "frustration" is generally taken to mean blocking or thwarting of some expected goal. A person, then, is frustrated if he expects to attain some goal but is prevented from doing so. "Aggression" is a form of behavior that is designed to injure another person

---

[13]This hypothesis has also been used by a number of other writers concerned with the problem of political violence. See, for example, Leonard Berkowitz, "Frustrations, Comparisons, and Other Sources of Emotion Arousal as Contributors to Social Unrest," *Journal of Social Issues,* 28:1 (1972), pp. 77–91; James Davies, "The J-Curve of Rising and Declining Satisfactions as a Cause of Some Great Revolutions and a Contained Rebellion," in *Violence in America,* ed. by Hugh Graham and Ted Gurr (New York: Bantam, 1969), pp. 547–76; and Ivo K. Feierabend and Rosalind L. Feierabend, "Aggressive Behavior Within Polities, 1948–1962: A Cross-National Study," *Journal of Conflict Resolution,* X:1 (March, 1966), pp. 249–71.

[14]It should be noted, however, that it is not accepted by all psychologists and that there are several variants, complete with varying definitions, of this hypothesis. For some evidence against the view that frustration leads to increased aggression, see William Gentry, "Effects of Frustration, Attack, and Prior Aggressive Training on Overt Aggression and Vascular Processes," *Journal of Personality and Social Psychology,* 16:4 (December, 1970), pp. 718–25.

[15]The frustration-aggression hypothesis is usually interpreted in stimulus-response terms, that is, a frustrating stimulus is thought to increase the probability of an aggressive response. As a stimulus, frustration is taken as an event external to the person being frustrated. It is not, in other words, a mental state characterizing the frustrated individual. Some authors do introduce a mental state, such an anger or arousal, as an intervening variable between frustration and aggression, but in terms of the general stimulus-response approach this type of procedure is not necessary.

[16]The probabilistic version of the frustration-aggression hypothesis seems to be the one that is currently accepted. Some stronger variants, however, have been proposed. For example, the classic version by John Dollard, *et al., Frustration and Aggression* (New Haven: Yale University Press, 1939) argued that aggression always stems from frustration.

or object. Note, however, that aggression need not be physical. According to at least one account, even hostile thoughts count as a form of aggression.[17]

A number of related hypotheses have been proposed about other factors that affect aggression. For example, aggression is thought to be more likely to occur if the frustration is viewed as arbitrary rather than justified. Other relevant factors are the prior reinforcement of aggression and/or the prior extinction of nonaggressive responses to frustration, which are also thought to increase the likelihood that a subject will respond aggressively to a frustrating stimulus. Finally, the intensity of aggression is thought to vary directly with the strength of frustration and inversely with the extent to which aggression is punished.[18]

Laboratory studies constitute the basic type of evidence used for the frustration-aggression and related hypotheses. Typically, the subject's aggression is measured by the intensity of the electrical shocks he is willing to inflict on some "victim" (who most fortunately never receives the shocks). Generally speaking, the evidence from these studies supports the view that the above factors affect the probability and intensity of aggression. In some cases, however, the evidence is questionable. For example, a curvilinear relationship between punishment and aggression is sometimes proposed. Laboratory studies have found an inverse linear relationship between these variables. It is not known, however, whether this finding simply results from the fact that the range of punishment appropriate for laboratory use is limited or whether the curvilinearity hypothesis is simply wrong.

The frustration-aggression hypothesis applies to individuals in interpersonal contexts.[19] One might attempt to generalize it to individuals in social settings, but such an attempt runs considerable risk of error. I shall try to show later that the fact that relative deprivation, unlike frustration, is a social phenomenon raises a number of problems that go beyond the scope of the frustration-aggression hypothesis. For the moment, it is sufficient to note that there is nothing in frustration-aggression studies that warrants generalizations to human behavior in different types of contexts.

---

[17]Leonard Berkowitz, "The Frustration-Aggression Hypothesis Revisited," in *Roots of Aggression*, ed. by Leonard Berkowitz (New York: Atherton, 1969), p. 3.

[18]See Leonard Berkowitz, *Aggression: A Social Psychological Analysis* (New York: McGraw-Hill, 1962); Russell Geen and David Stonner, "Reactions to Aggression," *The Journal of Psychology*, 83 (January, 1973), pp. 95–102; Paul D. Knott and Bruce A. Drost, "Effects of Varying Intensity of Attack and Fear Arousal on the Intensity of Counter Aggression," *Journal of Personality*, 40:1 (March, 1972), pp. 27–37; and Paul Rothaus and Philip Worchel, "The Inhibition of Aggression under Nonarbitrary Frustration," *Journal of Personality*, 28:1 (March, 1960), pp. 108–17.

[19]It has also been found to hold for animals. This point may be worth noting in that, although one hesitates to generalize from animal to human behavior, there seems little reason to expect the frustration-aggression relationship to be a purely culture-bound phenomenon.

The Forms of Political Violence

On Gurr's definition, political violence refers to "all collective attacks within a political community against the political regime, its actors—including competing political groups as well as incumbents—or its policies."[20] This definition is rather confusing. As Freeman sees it, the definition suggests inclusion of government aggression under the category of political violence.[21] There is little in Gurr's theory, however, to show that such acts fall within its scope. Furthermore, the term "attacks" is quite vague. "Aggression," in the frustration-aggression hypothesis, included hostile thoughts and verbal aggression as well as physical aggression. If we interpret attacks in this sense, such things as newspaper attacks, if written by two or more people, constitute a form of political violence. But, this does not seem to be what Gurr believes.

It might be easier to determine what Gurr has in mind when he refers to acts of political violence by simply examining his classification of the forms of political violence. Here we find that political violence is divided into three forms: internal war, turmoil, and conspiracy.[22] These general categories include such things as riots, coups, mutinies, guerrilla wars, revolutions, and civil wars. Apparently, when Gurr refers to political violence, he is referring to the kinds of acts that are commonly thought of as political violence and not to the type of act that would be considered aggression or the type of act indicated by his definition.

It is not, however, very common to classify acts of political violence into the three forms Gurr uses. Revolutions, for example, are often considered to be very distinctive phenomena that differ in fundamental ways from other types of political violence. In Gurr's theory, revolutions would be grouped together will all other relatively organized acts of political violence that involve widespread participation. It may be true that revolutions are indeed phenomena that are basically similar to other types of political violence. But this assertion requires some justification.

Gurr offers two main justifications for the use of his threefold classification.[23] The first is based on empirical investigations of the dimensions of

---

[20]Gurr, pp. 3–4.
[21]Freeman, "Review Article," p. 349.
[22]For definitions of these terms, see above, p. 53.
[23]Gurr also argues that his typology may be justified on the grounds that the various forms he distinguishes have different effects on political systems (p. 334). This justification, however, is

political violence. The second is that these three forms of political violence have distinguishable, although related, causes. The empirical justification for this typology is rather tenuous. Rudolph Rummel, to be sure, found that through the use of factor analysis, data on political violence could be reduced to three major dimensions.[24] But in replicating the Rummel study, Raymond Tanter found that acts of political violence could be reduced, with a roughly similar loss of information, to two major dimensions.[25] And, in a subsequent study based on Guttman scale analysis, Betty Nesvold found that acts of political violence could be reduced to a unidimensional scale.[26] These studies might, of course, be subjected to a number of methodological critiques. But this is not the issue here. What is important now is that all we can say about the dimensionality of political-violence data is that it is dependent on the particular data and techniques used in the analysis. There seems to be no justification for the assertion that acts of political violence empirically form three dimensions.

Gurr's theoretical justification in terms of the distinguishable causes of the three forms of political violence is much more interesting. Theoretical justifications for classifications are sometimes questioned on the grounds that the classifications become "theory-laden": the theory specifies the causes to be used in classifying phenomena that will then be explained by the theory. This poses no problem for me. We have long been aware that theories often contain provisions for measuring and organizing empirical phenomena. As long as this procedure does not result in the theory becoming completely irrefutable—which in this case it does not—there is little reason for concern.

However, on the causal justification, the use of *three* categories is completely arbitrary. Most of the variables used as determinants of the form of political violence are not discrete variables that can take on one of three values. Rather, they are generally interval variables. The ratio of dissident to regime coercive control, for example, ranges from complete equality to extreme inequality. Of course, convenient, if arbitrary, distinctions are often made in political science in order to facilitate analysis. The point here is simply that this classification does seem arbitrary. There is little justification, in either frustration-aggression analogies, empirical studies, or theoretical claims, for grouping acts of political violence under these three labels.

---

highly questionable. On Gurr's definitions, the Cuban Revolution would probably be classified as a conspiracy, whereas the French and Chinese Revolutions would be internal wars. Yet the effects of the Cuban and Chinese Revolutions seem far more similar than those of the French and Chinese Revolutions. See Freeman, "Review Article."

[24]Rummel, "Dimensions of Conflict Behavior."

[25]Raymond Tanter, "Dimensions of Conflict Behavior Within and Between Nations, 1958–60," *Journal of Conflict Resolution*, X:1 (March, 1966), pp. 41–64.

[26]Betty Nesvold, "Scalogram Analysis of Political Violence" in *Macro-Quantitative Analysis*, ed. by John V. Gillespie and Betty Nesvold (Beverly Hills, Calif.: Sage, 1971), pp. 167–86.

Relative Deprivation:
The Social Context

With one important qualification, the concept of relative deprivation is basically the social analogue to the concept of frustration. Relative deprivation was taken to be the "perceived discrepancy between men's values expectations and their value capabilities." Frustration is similarly conceived as the deprivation of an expected goal. Both concepts, in short, denote situations in which something is expected and not received. The major qualification is that whereas frustration is generally treated as an external stimulus, relative deprivation is defined in terms of *perceived* discrepancy, indicating that it is probably viewed as a mental concept. For purposes here, however, this difference is not crucial.

The similarity between the two definitions is somewhat misleading in that it masks important differences in what might be termed the theoretical contexts of these terms. Frustration is used in interpersonal contexts; relative deprivation, in social contexts. In many respects, the differences between the two contexts suggest that one cannot simply treat relative deprivation as entirely analogous to frustration.

Relative deprivation, first of all, is a concept that involves relations among individuals. The term apparently came into vogue when it became clear that absolute deprivation, or poverty, could not possibly be the cause of rebellion since the world is filled with poor people who obviously do not usually rebel. It seemed more likely that if deprivation were the answer, it would have to be deprivation of a relative nature, that is, induced by unfavorable social comparisons.

It seems reasonable to suppose that part of these comparisons are between the past and present status of a single individual or, in other words, that the conditions under which a person has lived in the past will affect his present expectations. It is equally reasonable to suppose that people will compare their own positions with those of others and base their expectations, to some extent, on comparisons with some "reference group." But here the problem becomes difficult. All people in a society are apparently not included in the reference group of an individual. Unless the theory is wrong, the poor presumably do not suffer severe relative deprivation by comparing their economic position with that of very wealthy individuals. But, if all people do not form a reference group, the problem becomes one of determining which people form that group. Gurr sees this problem—which does not arise in purely interpersonal contexts—but does not attempt to solve it.

In terms of a social theory the reference-group problem becomes crucial. Gurr devotes considerable attention to an analysis of the social origins of relative deprivation. Without a solution to the reference-group problem, however, such analysis is impossible. We cannot tell which societal conditions affect relative deprivation until we know how individuals react to changes in their own positions and in those of others. To use an example, without an analysis of the reference-group problem, there is no way to analyze the effects of economic decline on relative deprivation. A person in declining economic conditions may experience relative deprivation with respect to his former economic position, but experience no relative deprivation in comparing his position with that of others. Unless we know how such comparisons are to be made, there is no basis for assuming that certain changes in a society will lead to relative deprivation.

One might, of course, argue that the social origins of relative deprivation constitute a separate problem that need not be incorporated into a theory of political violence. This view, however, has two problems. The first is that the theory relies on the concept of relative deprivation to explain political violence, and the term relative clearly includes social comparisons. The nature of these social comparisons, then, is an issue that is closely related to the theory and might reasonably be included in it. The second problem is more practical and concerns the issue of testability. The extent of relative deprivation in a society is very difficult to determine through direct means. Studies that rely on concepts such as relative deprivation generally infer changes in relative deprivation from changes in societal conditions thought to be related to relative deprivation. This obviously presupposes an analysis of the social origins of relative deprivation. In the absence of this type of analysis the problem of testability is virtually insoluble.

A second issue that poses different problems for relative deprivation and frustration theories concerns the types of values that are relevant. "Values" here refer to those things that a person desires. In frustration-aggression studies it is usually tacitly assumed that the types of values with respect to which a person is frustrated do not affect the ensuing aggression.

One wonders, however, whether this assumption makes sense in a social context. Gurr distinguishes among three classes of values: welfare, power, and interpersonal values. These classes are then further subdivided into a number of subclasses. In and of itself, there is nothing wrong with this scheme. But it raises a number of issues, unfortunately left unanalyzed, when integrated into the general theory of political violence. It seems hardly reasonable to suppose that a person experiencing relative deprivation due to personal problems in his family will have the same propensity to engage in collective violence as a person whose relative deprivation is of the same intensity but arises from the fact that the government has turned off his water supply. It seems reasonable to suppose that some types of values are more relevant to collective violence than others.

We should also note that Gurr defines relative deprivation as the average discrepancy between what the individual expects to attain and what he feels capable of attaining under the status quo. But why should the emphasis be on *personal* deprivation? Many of the twentieth-century revolutionary leaders have been relatively well off, at least in economic terms. There is no indication that these men suffered from intense personal deprivation. If the term is applicable to them at all, it is more likely that the basis for their relative deprivation lay in their beliefs about the goods that other people should and would get in the society. So, feelings of social justice may be as relevant to political violence as beliefs about personal relative deprivation.[27]

Finally, a possible difference concerns the pattern of relative-deprivation development. Psychologists generally assume that it is the intensity of frustration rather than the pattern of its development that acts as the determinant of aggression. One might question whether this is true in the case of political violence. Gurr describes three patterns of relative-deprivation development but does not analyze possible differences in their effects on political violence.

At first glance, there is little reason to suspect that the pattern of relative-deprivation development would be important. If violence is caused by the *gap* between value expectations and value capabilities, it would not seem that different effects will result if that gap is caused by declining capabilities (decremental deprivation), increasing expectations (aspirational deprivation), or both (progressive deprivation).[28] A focus on the actual gap rather than the way it developed, however, was suggested by frustration-aggression studies. But these studies examine only the effects of nonfulfillment of expectations; they do not consider the effects of declining capabilities. If capabilities decrease considerably, people might simply be too concerned with the problem of survival to be able to expend their energy on political rebellion. Decremental deprivation, then, may lead to less political violence than the other patterns of relative-deprivation development. This is purely speculative. The issue is raised only because in this area as well there are plausible reasons for doubting the similarity between the frustration-aggression and the relative deprivation-political violence relationships.

---

[27]For a more detailed examination of this issue see David Bell, *Resistance and Revolution* (Boston: Houghton Mifflin, 1973) and Peter Lupsha, "Explanation of Political Violence: Some Psychological Theories versus Indignation," *Politics and Society,* 2:1 (Fall, 1971), pp. 89–104.

[28]Progressive deprivation is basically the J-curve model proposed by Davies. See James Davies, "Toward a Theory of Revolution," *American Sociological Review,* 27:1 (February, 1962), pp. 5–19 and "The J-Curve."

The above considerations do not indicate that studies of interpersonal aggression are irrelevant to studies of social violence. They do, however, suggest that these two phenomena might not be entirely analogous and that analyses of political violence might well involve considerations other than those involved in studies of interpersonal aggression. There is simply no reason to assume that an individual's behavior in a social context will be completely similar to his behavior in interpersonal contexts. In many cases, Gurr seems to assume a similarity between the two types of phenomena that may not be warranted.

The Level of Analysis Problem

The problem with using studies of frustration as a basis for a theory of political violence is further complicated by the fact that the frustration-aggression hypothesis, which Gurr takes as the causal mechanism underlying his theory, is a hypothesis about the behavior of individuals. But, the theory of political violence is a theory about the behavior of large groups of people. It states, basically, the conditions in a *society* that affect the magnitude of political violence experienced by the society. The difference between the two is crucial. There is no reason to suppose that individual behavior is in any way similar to group behavior or, saying it another way, that the behavior of people in large groups will follow the same laws as the behavior of isolated individuals.

This issue, it may be observed, is in no way relevant to the question of methodological individualism. Many social scientists have adopted the individualist position that all attributes of groups may be defined in terms of the individuals composing the group and the relations among these or that there are no emergent group properties. Some individualists even claim that, in principle, laws of group behavior may be reduced to (or explained in terms of) laws of individual behavior. Even the most extreme individualist, however, would not claim that laws of group behavior must be the *same* as laws of individual behavior. The assumption of explanatory individualism does not, for example, warrant the inference that if the frustration-aggression hypothesis holds true for individuals, it must hold true for groups. Nor does the assumption of definitional individualism warrant the assertion that group properties must be definable in terms of the attributes of the individual members alone. Relations among members of the group may be extremely important.[29]

---

[29]For a summary discussion of these issues, see May Brodbeck, "Methodological Individualism: Definition and Reduction" in *Readings,* ed. by May Brodbeck, pp. 180–303.

Gurr's discussion almost completely ignores the nature of intragroup relations. Relations among individuals are not incorporated into either the definitions of group phenomena or hypotheses about group behavior. The neglect of relations among individuals is particularly evident in Gurr's definition of the intensity of relative deprivation in a society as the *average* of the individual intensities. If individuals in a society acted independently, this definition would make a good deal of sense. But additive indices presuppose independence. If people interact so that the intensity of relative deprivation of one individual depends on the relative deprivation of others, there is no reason to suppose that an additive index is valid. On a strictly stipulative view of definitions, Gurr, of course, may use a word to mean exactly what he wishes it to mean. But, in theoretical terms, this definition makes little sense.

The problem of levels of analysis and interaction effects is not simply a pedantic issue raised by methodologists to bore everyone else. There is considerable evidence indicating that groups of people do not, in fact, behave in the same manner as isolated individuals. National data, for example, often reveal a relatively high ecological correlation between urbanization and political participation. There is, however, no correlation between urban residence and political participation at the individual level.[30] Those who are not convinced by theoretical arguments against making automatic inferences from individual to group behavior might at least be persuaded that in practice group behavior often differs considerably from the behavior of individuals.

It is true, of course, that to say that laws of group behavior are not always analogous to laws of individual behavior does not mean that there are no cases in which this analogy holds. One might argue that Gurr is claiming that such an analogy holds for the case of political violence, and thus far no evidence has been presented indicating that he is wrong. We might separate this claim into two components: that the frustration-aggression relationships hold for groups, and (and this is implicit in the definition of societal relative deprivation) that there are no interaction effects with respect to aggression among individuals in a group.

There is evidence indicating that the latter claim is erroneous. Laboratory findings show that not only does the presence of an "aggressive model" have an effect on the likelihood that a person will behave aggressively but also that when another person (the aggressive model) is present, the effects

[30]Norman Nie, G. Bingham Powell, Jr., and Kenneth Prewitt, "Social Structure and Political Participation: Developmental Relationships," in *Cross-National Micro-Analysis,* ed. by John Pierce and Richard Pride (Beverly Hills: Sage, 1972), pp. 135–97. For a theoretical discussion of the problem of ecological correlation, see Hayward R. Alker, Jr., "A Typology of Ecological Fallacies," in *Quantitative Ecological Analysis in the Social Sciences,* ed. by Mattei Dogan and Stein Rokkan (Cambridge: MIT, 1969), pp. 69–86; and Donald Stokes, "Cross-National Inference as a Game Against Nature," in *Mathematical Applications in Political Science* IV, ed. by Joseph L. Bernd (Charlottesville: University of Virginia Press, 1968), pp. 62–83.

of his influence cannot simply be added to the effects of frustration to predict the frequency of a subject's aggression. In other words, when more than one person is involved, the study of aggression does involve interaction effects.

It might, of course, be true that if we knew how to incorporate these effects into the analysis, we would be able to combine individual measures of relative deprivation into a societal measure of relative deprivation in such a way that the frustration-aggression relationship would also hold at the aggregate level. But this is a big "if"—one that is hardly satisfied by Gurr's analysis.

In conclusion, it seems fair to state that given a severe level of analysis problem, the frustration-aggression hypothesis cannot be automatically invoked to explain group phenomena.[31] Furthermore, in Gurr's study, the level of analysis problem is quite serious. Not only is there no justification for the assertion that the frustration-aggression hypothesis can be used to explain hypotheses about the magnitude of political violence, there is also no justification, on either theoretical or empirical grounds, for the implicit assumption that interaction effects among members of a group can be ignored in a theory of this type.

Selection of Variables

Gurr's analysis relies on more than 50 variables to explain political violence. This is perhaps not unreasonable since political violence is a complex phenomenon and, as such, might require an equally complex explanation. An adequate explanation, however, must not only specify relevant variables; there must also be some justification, preferably through the use of an additional theory that explains the posited relationships among variables, for regarding the specified variables as causal factors rather than spurious correlates. A requirement of this sort was deemed necessary since social-science data are often widely intercorrelated, and it is difficult (if not impossible) to eliminate spurious factors on empirical grounds alone.[32] The purpose of this section is to examine the justifications for including the variables used in Gurr's theory.

It may be useful in this respect to recall how this problem was handled by the much simpler rational-choice theory of participation. Here the variables singled out as being relevant to an individual's decision to participate in

---

[31] It might, however, be possible to use the frustration-aggression hypothesis in a reduction of a theory of group violence to one of individual violence, but this again presupposes knowledge of combinations and relations that is not available at present.

[32] There are, of course, statistical tests for spuriousness, but these presuppose assumptions that are often far from satisfied.

collective action were the presence of selective incentives and the possibility that the individual's actions would have a noticeable impact on the provision of the collective good. As these were defined, both variables resulted in chages in the relative utilities of the alternative courses of action open to the individual. The relevance of these variables may then be easily explained through utility theory since, by the assumptions of this theory, changes in the relative utilities of different courses of action result in changes in the course of action chosen by the individual.

In Gurr's theory, as in other psychological theories of this type, the analogue to utility theory is the frustration-aggression hypothesis. The frustration-aggression hypothesis, however, does not *explain* why the variables included in the theory are related to political violence. Rather, it serves as an *analogy*. The basic idea here seems to be as follows: Political violence is similar in many respects to interpersonal aggression; therefore, the variables that affect political violence should be similar to the variables that affect aggression. Implicit here is some assumption that similar effects have similar causes.

It is not difficult to see that many of the variables used in Gurr's theory are analogous to variables used in psychological studies of aggression. Relative deprivation is similar to frustration; past success of violence, to reinforcement. We might also consider coercion as similar to punishment and legitimacy as fairly similar to the arbitrary-nonarbitrary nature of the frustration variable used in psychological studies of aggression.

The uses of analogy have been hotly debated. Some people would claim that analogies can only suggest variables, but can never validate or justify the inclusion of these variables. Others believe that analogies do serve to justify inclusion of variables by showing that similar variables have been incorporated in similar ways in another, more developed theory. As a reasonable compromise, I would suggest that analogies do give us some reason to believe that the variables are not spurious, although this type of justification is weaker than that provided by an explanatory theory. However, the justification provided by this type of procedure can only be as good as the analogy on which it rests. In other words, the strength of the analogy is very important: strong analogies may provide some justification for the inclusion of variables in a theory, but analogies that are very weak cannot serve this purpose.

In examining the strength of the analogy between the frustration-aggression hypotheses and Gurr's relative-deprivation theory, we are again confronted with the level of analysis and social-context problems. That in one case we are dealing with individuals in interpersonal situations and, in the other, with groups in social and political situations makes the analogy rather tenuous. Political violence is similar to interpersonal aggression only in that both involve the deliverance of a "noxious stimulus." But the contexts in the two cases are very different, and the similarity breaks down not only because in one case the phenomenon involves interacting individuals, while in the other it does not, but also because the objects against which violence is directed are personal in the case of aggression, and impersonal or remote in the case of political violence. Similar considerations hold for the other analogies between variables. Given these problems, the justification for including variables on the basis of their analogy with psychological variables used in hypotheses about aggression is, at best, rather weak.

The problem of justifying the inclusion of variables is further complicated by the fact that not all of the variables Gurr uses are analogous to those used in frustration-aggression hypotheses. Many are included on the basis that other people have considered them important, and they seem to be plausible causes of political violence. For example, the nature of institutional support for the regime and the rebels readily appears as a plausible factor affecting the magnitude of political violence, although there is nothing in psychological studies of aggression that would suggest this.

Plausibility considerations are, I think, extremely weak justifications for including variables. The simple fact of the matter is that we can think of hundreds of plausible factors affecting political violence. Unless we have some way of determining which variables are important and, for that matter, how they should be related to other variables, there is no way to justify excluding some variables as relevant factors. There are many variables that are not included in this study that seem at least as plausible as the ones that are included. For example, foreign governments often use a variety of measures, ranging from aid to military intervention, to bolster a tottering regime, and it would seem reasonable to suppose that these measures would affect the nature of political violence. A second factor that seems plausible but is not analyzed by Gurr concerns the role of the intellectuals in political violence. Given sufficient imagination, I am sure that many more plausible factors could be uncovered. If all plausible factors were used, our analyses of political violence would probably include more variables than cases. Plausibility considerations, in short, are too open; they can be used to justify the inclusion of virtually anything and consequently manage to exclude very little.

Due to problems with both analogies and plausibility considerations, the justification for including variables in Gurr's theory is extremely weak. This is one of the major shortcomings of this theory. In the absence of such justification, there is no reason to believe that Gurr's theory does not provide us with a list of spurious correlates rather than an explanation of political violence.

Empirical Findings

Gurr's theory has a number of theoretical problems. However, he presents us with a wealth of evidence to support his hypotheses, and if this evidence is satisfactory, his work will have at least served the purpose of uncovering empirical relationships in political-violence data. This is not a negligible contribution. Analyses of revolutions and political violence would undoubtedly be greatly facilitated if more were known about the empirical relationships among variables. To see whether Gurr's work may be helpful in this area, we must investigate the types of evidence he uses and determine if this evidence provides adequate support for the hypotheses he presents.

The evidence adduced to support hypotheses is fairly problematical. As in every other theory in the social sciences, we run into the problem of empirical referents. Gurr's hypotheses, of course, are stated in theoretical terms. Such things as "value expectations" are not directly observable in any sense of the word. To test hypotheses containing such terms, we need something like "correspondence rules" or measurement techniques that will link the theoretical expressions to things we can observe in the real world. But adequate rules or techniques of this sort are generally unavailable. The most common practice in testing political theories is to use some indicator that is admittedly imperfect but seems to be as good as anything else we can think of. This is basically the practice followed by Gurr. While such a procedure seems warranted in view of the difficulty of devising better ways to handle this problem, it should be noted that this introduces problems in evaluating evidence since in many cases we have good reason to believe that the indicators are rather inadequate measures.

Gurr uses two main types of evidence to support his hypotheses: case studies of political violence and statistical studies of cross-national data. Both have some problems, but both may be used to provide us with some evidence for or against these hypotheses.

The case-study evidence is problematical for two reasons. The first is that, in a sense, it involves a backward testing procedure. The general procedure for using case studies is: given a hypothesis of the form "if a, then b," examine an instance of a and see if it is also an instance of b. In examining instances of political violence, however, the tests are actually examining an instance of "b" to see if it is also an "a."

To illustrate this point, let us examine evidence for a hypothesis relating relative deprivation to political rebellions. Although Gurr is not explicit about which hypothesis he is testing with this evidence, it is presumably something to the effect that "severe relative deprivation in a society is likely to lead to political rebellion." One case used to support this view is Dorr's Rebellion, a rebellion in Rhode Island in 1842.[33] This rebellion was preceded by a long period of economic improvement and expanding political benefits followed by a short reversal period consisting of an economic depression and the denial of a future extension of political suffrage. The economic and political trends here are taken to be indicative of severe relative deprivation.

This evidence, to be sure, provides us with a case of political rebellion preceded by what we may take to be a case of severe relative deprivation. But the focus on cases of political violence rather than the antecedent conditions obscures as much as it enlightens. We know that there are several cases in which economic depressions—which are presumably indicative of relative deprivation—were not followed by major political upheavals. In order to test the above hypothesis, we need to know whether such upheavals are more likely to occur when there is severe relative deprivation than when this condition is not present. To do this, we would have to examine cases of societies with and without severe relative deprivation and determine how many of each had subsequent political upheavals. Of course, if many cases of political rebellions were examined, and each was found to be preceded by severe relative deprivation, we might suspect that this factor does indeed affect the likelihood of rebellions. But this procedure introduces an additional source of error into an area that is already filled with hazardous inferences.

The second problem of case-study evidence is that the hypotheses are probabilistic, and a case that does not conform to the hypotheses cannot disconfirm it. The use of this type of procedure, then, becomes one-sided: if a case conforms to the hypothesis, it is presented as confirming evidence; if it does not, it does not provide disconfirming evidence since the hypothesis does not rule out such cases but only states that they are rather unlikely to occur. Since the hypotheses are probabilistic, it would be more appropriate to use some form of statistical inference, at least on a very low level to allow for consideration of such things as differences in the proportions of cases. This type of procedure might, for example, be used to compare cases of societies with and without severe relative deprivation to determine which group exhibited a greater frequency of political violence.

There are, of course, a variety of statistical techniques, some of which are more appropriate than others in investigating this problem. The statistical evidence presented by Gurr is almost entirely based on the use of the simple Pearsonian product-moment correlation coefficient. This is a linear measure

---

[33]This evidence was originally presented by Davies, "The J-Curve," in support of his theory of revolutions.

of association designed to determine the size and direction of the relationship between two variables. There are a variety of problems associated with the use of this statistic to test Gurr's hypotheses, not the least of which is that the correlation coefficient is a linear measure of association, whereas these hypotheses do not postulate linear relationships between the variables. This poses a problem similar to that involved in the use of case studies. If the correlation is high, we may take it as confirming evidence for the hypothesis (since a line is a monotonic function and the hypotheses do specify monotonicity). However, if the correlation is very low, we can only say that the relationship is nonlinear; for all we know the data might well be represented by some other monotonic function. Of course, we might claim that if the function is in fact monotonic, it should be approximated by a linear function, so that if the correlation is very close to zero, we would have reason to view the hypothesis as being disconfirmed. But this also involves rather hazardous inferences.

A second problem with Gurr's use of correlation coefficients is that virtually all are simple bivariate correlations. The theory, however, includes more than two variables. In other words, the theory specifies that one of the assumptions underlying the use of correlation coefficients—that all relevant variables are included in the equation—is violated for the case of bivariate correlations. Under these conditions, bivariate correlation coefficients are often misleading measures of the strength of the association between two variables: They may be highly inflated if the relationship between the two variables is largely spurious or even deflated if a third uncontrolled variable is masking the "true" effects. In short, unless there is good reason to believe that there is only one relevant independent variable or that all of the independent variables are uncorrelated with each other, it is unwise to rely on bivariate correlations. Multiple regression and partial correlation coefficients are designed to take care of this type of problem and can provide better estimates of the nature of the association between two variables.

Fortunately, some partial correlation and regression coefficients have been computed, and these may be used to indicate whether we have made a mountain out of a molehill in stressing the dangers of inferences based on bivariate correlations or whether this problem is indeed serious. One of the variables used by Gurr as an immediate determinant of the magnitude of political violence is institutionalization, or the extent to which social structures are broad in scope, complex, and adaptable. Gurr hypothesizes that this variable (which is roughly equivalent to the regime-institutional-support variable in the diagrams in the Appendix) is negatively associated with the magnitude of political violence. And, it is: the bivariate correlation is −.33, a figure that is not outstandingly high but nevertheless in the right direction and of a more or less respectable magnitude. However, the partial-correlation coefficient, computed by controlling for the effects of seven other independent variables, is .07—a figure that is not only exceedingly low but also in the wrong direction. A similar phenomenon occurs with regime coercive potential, another immediate determinant of the magnitude of political violence. The bivariate correlation here is −.51, while the partial is only −.17—a coefficient that is in the right direction but of considerably lower magnitude.[34] These results indicate, I believe, that the problem of interpreting bivariate correlations may be serious.

This finding also indicates that there is another problem with Gurr's theory. Partial correlation coefficients only differ from bivariate ones when the two or more independent variables are intercorrelated. But Gurr does not focus much attention on the interrelationships among his independent or explanatory variables. This problem would not be severe were it not for the fact that some plausible relationships suggest that we are actually dealing with a nonrecursive system. (A nonrecursive system is one that exhibits "circular causation" so that it takes a form such as: x is dependent on y, y is dependent on z, and z is dependent on x.) For example, we might suppose that a regime's coercive strength would be dependent to some extent on the magnitude of political violence in a society since if violence increases or is expected to increase, a regime might well devote more of its resources to coercive-control facilities. However, as Freeman notes, utilitarian justifications for political violence are probably heavily dependent on the extent to which regime forces are capable of crushing dissident forces.[35] To complete the loop, we have only to observe that Gurr hypothesizes that utilitarian justifications for political violence affect the potential for political violence, which, in turn, affects the magnitude of political violence. If the system is, in fact, nonrecursive, the Ordinary Least Squares estimation procedures underlying standard regression and correlation analysis are unwarranted.[36]

There is some evidence indicating that variables relevant to political violence do constitute a nonrecursive system. This is based on two recent studies of political violence that use nonrecursive or reciprocal estimation techniques to analyze the interdependencies among variables commonly used to explain political violence.[37] Both studies found significant reciprocal

[34]These findings are reported in Ted Gurr, "A Causal Model of Civil Strife: A Comparison Analysis Using New Indices," *American Political Science Review*, LXII:4 (December, 1968), pp. 1104–24.

[35]Freeman, "Review Article," p. 353.

[36]For an excellent and very simple discussion of this see Ronald and Thomas Wonnacott, *Econometrics* (New York: Wiley, 1970), pp. 149–95 and 337–400.

[37]Ted Robert Gurr and Raymond Duvall, "Civil Conflict in the 1960's A Reciprocal Theoretical System with Parameter Estimates" *Comparative Political Studies*, 6:2 (July, 1973) pp. 135–69; and Hibbs, *Mass Political Violence*.

effects among such variables. Unfortunately, this result is virtually the only one these studies had in common. There was little overlap in the substantive conclusions the authors drew about the variables and interrelationships that form the political violence system. It would appear, then, that variables relevant to political violence may be interrelated in complex, nonrecursive ways; however, the precise nature of these interactions remains largely speculative.

When all is said and done, the problem of evaluating the evidence as a whole remains. Although there are a variety of problems with the evidence, no one expects testing procedures in political science to be unproblematical. And to say that the evidence is questionable is not to say that it is worthless. Gurr presents a wide variety of evidence based on different data and different types of testing procedures. Although each piece of evidence is of questionable value, taken as a whole the evidence does seem to support the view that there are empirical associations among the hypothesized variables. The extent of these associations, however, seems to range from weak to moderate. None of the evidence supports the view that there are very strong relationships among the variables. It seems probable that some, but not all, of the hypothesized relationships are spurious, while others involve more complex interrelationships than the theory would suggest.

Conclusion

In a sense, Gurr's theory embodies the dilemma of theories of revolution. Although psychological motivations appear to be very important factors in explaining why people become revolutionaries, they are also very elusive and difficult to incorporate into social theories. It is hard enough to determine how such factors operate in isolated settings. The contextual effects that must invariably be incorporated into the analysis of social issues make this task all the more difficult.

It is not surprising, then, that Gurr's theory fails to meet the established criteria for explanatory adequacy. The theory does, of course, specify the relevant variables that affect the magnitude and form of political violence. But the psychological theory that is used to supply the core assumptions cannot explain how or why these variables are relevant to political violence. Thus, it is never clear whether the theory explains revolutions and related forms of political violence or merely provides us with a list of spurious correlates of these phenomena. Evidence presented in support of the theory only confirms this judgment. When all of the methodological problems with this evidence are taken into account, the most that can be said is that there is some moderate degree of association among variables. Whether this is due to spurious correlations, failure to consider relevant variables, neglect of relevant interrelationships among the variables, or various other methodological problems remains an open question.

Perhaps the problem with this theory is simply that it is too ambitious. Gurr is attempting to explain why some societies experience more political violence than others by relying on a subsidiary explanation of individual rebellion that, in turn, relies on psychological theories of interpersonal aggression. This is a long chain. In order to move from a theory of interpersonal aggression to one of individual political rebellion, it is first necessary to determine the effects of the social context on people's basic aggressive tendencies. Then, in moving from a theory of individual rebellion to one of political violence in societies, we must determine the composition laws relating individual to group behavior. It would probably be easier, and ultimately more satisfactory, to begin by focusing exclusively on the first step and use the frustration-aggression hypothesis as a basis for explaining why people participate in acts of political violence. Once this issue has been adequately resolved, it may then be possible to use these explanations of individual rebellion in conjunction with theories of group behavior to develop a theory of political violence in societies. In this way, the major problems that beset Gurr's theory could be tackled in relative isolation from each other.

These tasks, of course, are not ones that can be easily resolved. Nevertheless, the importance of the issues involved makes such attempts well worth the effort. Gurr's theory has considerable intuitive appeal. The idea that relative deprivation, mediated by such factors as government legitimacy, the efficacy of past violence, and the strength of the rebel movement, induces political rebellion makes a great deal of sense. The basic conception of the theory, then, may well be sound. What it lacks is a good psychological basis that can incorporate the complex social and institutional relationships that affect the nature of political violence in a society.

IV

revolution and
the disequilibrated
social system

Both rational-choice and social-psychological theories rely on motivational
assumptions to explain revolutions. The rational-choice theory assumes that
people always reach decisions in a certain way and then examines how this
method of decision-making might induce people to participate in revolutionary movements. Similarly, social-psychological theories begin by assuming a certain psychology of individual rebellion and then extend these notions
to the social realm in order to explain political rebellion. In both cases, the
explanatory focus is on the individual: roughly speaking, the theories explain
revolutions by explaining why people become motivated to rebel against the
existing political order.

   This procedure makes some sense. Revolutions, after all, cannot occur
unless people decide to make them. Explanations of individual rebellion,
then, constitute a basic component in explanations of the phenomenon of
revolutions. At the same time, revolutions are not an individual-level

phenomenon: countries, rather than people, have revolutions. Furthermore, since revolutions are social rather than purely individual phenomena, it is reasonable to suppose that the structural characteristics of a given society affect an individual's decision to join a revolutionary movement and, in turn, the likelihood that the society will experience a revolution. This means that revolutions can also be analyzed at the societal level by focusing on the conditions in a society that are likely to give rise to revolutionary movements.

Ideally, a theory of revolutions would analyze both motivational and structural factors affecting revolutions and explain how the two are interrelated. A theory that successfully accomplished this task could then explain why people participate in revolutionary movements, why large-scale revolutions occur in some societies, and how individual participation is linked with the outbreak of revolutions. In short, such a theory could explain all aspects related to the causes of revolutions.

At this stage, however, most theories of revolution do not attempt to explain all aspects of the revolutionary process, and even those that do tend to rely on either motivational or structural assumptions, but not both. The assumptions used by Gurr and Olson, for example, focused exclusively on motivational factors. The remaining theories that will be considered are constructed around structural assumptions as to the nature of societies and social change. Johnson's theory is concerned exclusively with the process of social change and completely ignores motivational factors affecting individual behavior.[1] Marx treats the revolutionary process at both the societal and the individual levels, but largely relies on assumptions about the contextual effects of social structures to explain individual behavior. Although structural assumptions will probably never be a completely viable alternative to motivational ones, they do supplement these by explaining revolutions from a different and potentially useful perspective.

The particular structural assumptions used by Johnson stem from the type of systems analysis used in General Systems Theory and structural-functionalism. This approach is quite controversial. Proponents claim that General Systems Theory provides the basis for a universal paradigm that will integrate all scientific (and social-scientific) disciplines under a common rubric.[2] Opponents argue that, at least in the social sciences, this variety of systems analysis—particularly when used in conjunction with functionalist assumptions—yields little more than empty jargon.[3]

One of the major reasons for this controversy is that many people employ-

---

[1] Johnson, *Revolutionary Change.* All citations to Johnson refer to this work.
[2] See, for example, Kenneth E. Boulding, "General Systems Theory–The Structure of Science," in *Modern Systems Research,* ed. by Buckley, pp. 3–10; and Ludwig von Bertalanffy, *General Systems Theory* (New York: George Braziller, 1968), pp. 30–8.
[3] Some of the major discussions of this issue are included in A. James Gregor, "Political Science

ing this type of approach are vague about the assumptions they use. Johnson's theory, unfortunately, is no exception. This makes evaluation more difficult since in order to evaluate the theory, it is first necessary to extract the assumptions on which the theory is based. In Johnson's case, however, this can be done with reasonable ease, posing no major problem. After presenting a brief overview of Johnson's theory, I will discuss some of the major concepts of systems analysis and describe the type of system Johnson seems to assume. Johnson's theory will then be evaluated in view of the assumptions of this particular type of theory. Although this procedure involves some risk of error, there are, I shall argue, good reasons for supposing that other plausible sets of assumptions would not change my evaluation and, consequently, for supposing that the evaluation is sound. Finally, I will discuss the problems of testability posed by the theory and consider some types of evidence that might be used to evaluate the empirical adequacy of the theory.

Revolution and the Homeostatic System:
An Overview

The basic assumption underlying Johnson's theory is that social systems are homeostatic, that is, they are "self-regulating." In the following section the notion of a homeostatic system will be discussed in greater detail. For the present, it is sufficient to note that the homeostatic system is open, that is, it receives inputs from its environment. Furthermore, the system influences environmental conditions and does so in a way designed to maintain the stability of the system.

The notion of systemic stability, or homeostatic equilibrium, is somewhat complicated. Systems analysts postulate the existence of certain "functional prerequisites," "essential variables," or "needs" that must be satisfied if a system is to survive or remain in adequate working order.[4] System stability,

---

and the Uses of Functional Analysis," *American Political Science Review,* LXII:2 (June, 1968), pp. 425–39; Carl Hempel, "The Logic of Functional Analysis" in *Aspects,* pp. 297–330; Martin Landau, *Political Theory and Political Science* (New York: Macmillan, 1972), pp. 103–46; Richard Rudner, *Philosophy of Social Science* (N.J.: Prentice-Hall, 1966), pp. 84–111; and Jerome Stephens, "The Logic of Functional and Systems Analyses in Political Science," *Midwest Journal of Political Science,* XIII: 3 (May, 1969), pp. 367–94.

[4] In more formal analyses, the "functional prerequisites" or "essential variables," as they are more commonly called, are simply stipulated. In other words, the analyst *defines* the system with respect to these variables. The system, then, survives by definition if the values of the essential variables remain within their "critical limits." Social scientists rarely adopt this stipulation procedure but try instead to determine some empirical prerequisites for system survival. This task is obviously very difficult, and at present there seems to be no common consensus regarding the functional prerequisites of societies. For all practical purposes, then, the social scientist, although he may not want to admit it, is basically stipulating a set of needs characterizing a system.

or homeostatic equilibrium, is then achieved when the system operates in such a manner that these functional prerequisites are satisfied.[5] In other words, a homeostatic system is in equilibrium when the values of the essential variables remain within the range necessary for the system to be in adequate working order.

Johnson adopts Parson's classification of the needs of social systems. According to this view, there are four functional prerequisites of society: socialization or pattern maintenance, adaptation to the environment, goal attainment, and integration and social control.[6] Socialization, of course, refers to the inculcation in children of societal values and norms. Adaptation includes such things as the differentiation and allocation of roles and the distribution of scarce resources. Goal attainment involves the formation and development of policies for achieving goals. Social control, finally, refers to the way in which problems of conflict and deviancy are prevented and, when they arise, solved.

These functional prerequisites are not the only ones that might be postulated. Other social scientists have assumed different functional prerequisites of social systems. A system that is in homeostatic equilibrium with respect to the functional prerequisites used by Johnson, then, might not be in homeostatic equilibrium with respect to the functional prerequisites adopted by other authors. What is essential here is that in terms of structural-functional analysis, it makes little sense to say that a system is or is not in homeostatic equilibrium. A system can only be considered to be stable or in equilibrium with respect to particular variables or functional prerequisites.[7] This point would be fairly trivial were it not for the fact that it is often overlooked, and the failure to recognize the relative nature of the concept of homeostatic equilibrium has resulted in considerable confusion.

When a homeostatic system is in adequate working order, it can successfully adapt to changes in environmental conditions. If environmental conditions change, the system will also change so as to maintain stability with respect to the functional prerequisites. Sometimes, however, conditions change so radically that the system is not capable of sufficient change, and the functional prerequisites are not satisfied, or, in other words, the essential variables take on values outside the range of system stability. When this occurs, the system, in Johnson's terminology, is said to be disequilibrated. The disequilibrated social system, according to Johnson, is a necessary

---

[5] The terms stability and equilibrium have other, more technical meanings in formal treatments of systems analysis. The definitions here are only intended to convey Johnson's usage.
[6] For a discussion of these, see Johnson, pp. 51–53.
[7] This point is emphasized by E. Nagel, "A Formalization of Functionalism," in *Systems Thinking*, ed. by F. E. Emery (Baltimore: Penguin, 1969), pp. 297–329. There is, of course, no harm in

condition for revolutions: a revolution can only take place in a disequilibrated social system.

The cause of disequilibrium in social systems, Johnson claims, is the dissynchronization between values and the social division of labor.[8] Presumably, this refers to a situation in which the predominant values in a society do not support the existing division of labor. In other words, the situation is one in which social values concerning the ethical division of labor in a society are widely divergent from the actual division of labor.

At this point, the theory becomes somewhat confusing. The most reasonable interpretation appears to be that when values and the social division of labor becomes dissynchronized, causing the system to become disequilibrated, either the system will undergo structural change, or it will be maintained solely through the use of force. A disequilibrated social system will either be structurally transformed, or it will become a police state.[9]

Johnson apparently believes that there are two major ways in which structural transformation can occur: it can be the result of "conservative change" initiated by the elite, or it can occur through revolutionary change. If the elite does not initiate conservative change, remaining intransigent, the confidence of the "nondeviant" actors in the capacity of the system to move toward resynchronization will evaporate. The resulting loss of authority serves as the second necessary condition for revolutions.

Dynamic considerations are quite important here. The disequilibrated social system, in Johnson's theory, cannot lead to revolution immediately. A revolution can only occur *after* a loss of authority has developed, that is, after the elite has failed to develop policies to relieve the dissynchronization. In other words, following dissynchronization, the disequilibrated system can either move to a police state, or the elite can implement conservative change. (Some combination of these two may also be possible if the elite uses additional force while it is implementing change.) This situation lasts for an unspecified amount of time. After this time has elapsed, if the elite has failed to develop new policies, it will suffer a loss of authority, and revolution becomes an imminent possibility.

---

saying that a system is in homeostatic equilibrium if there is no confusion regarding the variables with respect to which the system is in equilibrium.

[8]Sometimes Johnson uses value–environmental dissynchronization instead of value-social division of labor dissynchronization. Since these two expressions appear to be used interchangeably, they are presumably equivalent.

[9]Johnson does not seem to allow for a third possibility that is sometimes used by functionalist authors: decay. However, Johnson does suggest that police states are not likely to survive longer than a single generation. If at the end of this period structural transformation has still not taken place, it is not clear what happens. Possibly, though, the concept of decay or disintegrating social systems might be introduced to cover this contingency.

79

The final condition for revolution is some "accelerator" that either deprives the elite of its coercive powers or leads revolutionaries to believe that they have the ability to deprive the elite of its coercive powers.[10] Johnson distinguishes among three types of accelerators.[11] The first includes all events that directly affect the loyalty of the armed forces. The most important of these is defeat in war, an event that in the presence of the other preconditions for revolution tends to turn the army against the existing political authorities. The remaining types of accelerators refer to phenomena that are usually associated with the revolution itself, rather than its causes.[12] One is the revolutionaries' belief that they can succeed; the other is any event initiated by revolutionaries against the armed forces. This conception of the nature of accelerators will be examined in detail later. For the present, it is enough to say that Johnson's "accelerators" include such things as the onset of guerrilla war, as well as traditional measures of precipitating factors.

The theory, briefly, is that given a disequilibrated system and elite intrasigence, a revolution will occur if some accelertor occurs. For the most part, Johnson adopts Bauer's definition of revolution: "Revolutions are social changes, successful or unsuccessful, involving violence and concerning the basic constitution of a society." [13] A successful revolution would implement structural change and restore system stability. But what of an unsuccessful revolution? Johnson does not discuss what happens in this case. Presumably, though, the system remains disequilibrated, and either a police state, conservative change by the elite, or a new revolution could develop.

The above definition of "revolution," however, is used for only part of Johnson's theory. In the latter part of his book, Johnson defines "revolution" as an insurrection whose ideology aims at recasting the social division of labor in an unprecedented way.[14] The two definitions are presumably not equivalent, as Johnson tells us that the theory as developed above holds for both revolutions (in the sense in which the term is used in the latter part of the book) and rebellions.[15]

Possibly what Johnson has in mind is that events denoted by "revolution" under the first definition (revolution₁) include those denoted by "revolution" under the second definition (revolution₂) as well as other insurrectionary

---

[10]The accelerator, Johnson claims, is "usually contributed by fortune." Freeman, "Review Article," p. 348, raises an interesting question about this formulation: "Who contributes it on the unusual occasions?"

[11]Johnson, pp. 99–105.

[12]For a critique of this see Freeman, "Review Article," p. 347.

[13]Arthur Bauer, *Essai sur les Révolutions* (Paris: Giard and Briere, 1908), p. 11, cited in Johnson, p. 1 (my translation).

[14]Johnson, pp. 140–41.

[15]Johnson, p. 136.

events or rebellions.[16] If this interpretation is accepted, then the theory as presented above holds for revolution$_1$. If the conditions for revolution$_1$ are present, either revolution$_2$ will occur, or rebellion will occur.

Johnson suggests that the conditions under which revolution$_2$, as opposed to rebellion, will occur are related to the structure of a society. Specifically, he argues that revolution$_2$ is more likely to occur in a functionally specific or differentiated society, whereas functionally diffuse societies are more likely to have rebellions. This analysis, however, is not carried very far, and Johnson emphasizes its tentative nature.[17] Since the analysis in this part is so sketchy, I will only examine the causes of revolution$_1$.

In summary, the theory basically states that the cause of revolution$_1$ is a set of conditions that includes: (1) a disequilibrated social system, (2) a loss of authority due to elite intrasigence, and (3) an accelerator. The causes of revolution$_2$ include those that cause revolution$_1$. In addition, however, the functional specificity of a society is statistically relevant for revolution$_2$, that is, given the above conditions, revolution$_2$ rather than rebellion is likely to occur if the society is functionally specific.

Systems Analysis and the Homeostatic Society

Systems analysts have developed a language all their own. The basic concepts are not difficult to understand. However, confusion sometimes arises because different authors use different terminology. Furthermore, there is a wide variety of systems that operate according to different principles. To avoid confusion, it is important to be explicit about the major concepts used in systems analysis and the particular assumptions made about different kinds of systems.

In its most general sense, a system is simply a set of interrelated variables. In open systems—which are the most common kind used in the social sciences—other, nonsystemic or environmental variables, as they are called, affect the value of the systemic variables. Technically, the distinction between system and environment is analytical. The investigator simply stipulates the variables that are to be included in the "system" and leaves

---

[16]This interpretation is somewhat problematical. Johnson claims that violence can occur even in a society that is in homeostatic equilibrium, but this type of violence is to be sharply distinguished from violence occurring in a disequilibrated society. However, if rebellions are included under "revolution," it is difficult to see how this can be done. Possibly what Johnson has in mind is some distinction of scale: If the system is in equilibrium, violence should be restricted to a small group of "deviants," whereas if the system is disequilibrated, widespread violence should result.
[17]Johnson, pp. 145–47.

others in the "environment." Of course, in many cases the distinction between system and environment can be made on a somewhat more natural basis. This is particularly true of many biological and chemical systems. In political science, however, the delineation of a system often has a rather strong arbitrary component.

The structure characterizing a system is the set of equations that give the functional relationships among systemic variables and between these variables and those of the environment. Virtually all social systems are dynamic, that is, they involve considerations of change over time. In the case of dynamic systems, the structure of a system usually takes the form of a set of differential or difference equations.

One particular type of open and dynamic system—the kind most frequently used by political scientists and sociologists—is the homeostatic system. This type of system involves some process of negative feedback or self-maintenance with respect to some trait or traits. The traits with respect to which the system is self-maintaining are alternatively referred to as the essential variables, functional prerequisites, or needs of the system. In order for the system to be considered in adequate working order, the values of these essential variables must remain within certain predetermined critical limits.

All this, of course, is general. We might, following the practice of most social scientists, assume that social and political systems are homeostatic. But homeostatic systems are not all alike. In particular, if we are to characterize social systems as homeostatic, we must decide how many feedback loops are involved. The issue here, to oversimplify somewhat, is whether we wish to portray social systems as adaptive systems capable of structural change (a system involving at least two feedback loops) or as simple homeostatic systems capable only of self-maintenance within a given structure (a system involving a single feedback loop).[18]

Before discussing these systems in greater detail, we should note that the usual characterization of a system in terms of its mathematical structure may be replaced by another characterization that is probably more feasible for political scientists to adopt. Although this characterization requires us to introduce additional concepts, it seems worthwhile to spend time on these. Political scientists cannot, at present, make informed speculations about the mathematical structure of an entire social system. If systems are characterized in terms of their structure, we are forced to treat the social system as a "black box." Although many political scientists do this, it is not, I believe, a

---

[18]For a discussion of social systems as ones capable of structural change, see Walter Buckley, "Society as a Complex Adaptive System," in *Modern Systems Research*, pp. 490–513.

particularly useful way to proceed, nor need it be the only way that systems analysis may be applied to political problems.

Ashby has suggested that many complex systems that cannot be represented in terms of their structure might be characterized by their fields.[19] The concept of a field of a system is fairly simple. At any given time, a system will be in some specific state in which the state of the system is simply the set of values taken on by the systemic variables at that time. In dynamic systems, the state of a system will change over time. Thus, we may develop a line of behavior that specifies the succession of states over time and the time intervals between. Suppose we were to develop lines of behavior for all possible initial states of a system in a particular set of environmental conditions. This would constitute the field of the system. Clearly, if we knew the structure of the system, we could derive its field. The converse, however, is not true. In other words, the characterization of a system in terms of its fields requires less knowledge about the system than does the structural characterization.

Now consider the behavior of a system with two feedback loops. This is the type of system Ashby designates as "ultrastable."[20] This system may be diagrammed as follows:

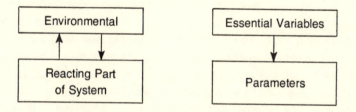

For political scientists, the environment would contain variables not included in the political system that affect the political system. The essential variables are designated by the analyst. For Johnson, these include socialization, adaptation, goal attainment, and social control. The reacting part in a political system would most probably be the behavior of the government or political elite. Finally, the parameters of a given system govern changes of field. This notion should become clearer as we investigate the way in which the system works.

[19]For a more complete discussion of this and the issues considered in the remainder of this section, see W. Ross Ashby, *Design for a Brain* (London: Science Paperbacks, 1960). Some of the definitions Ashby uses are not equivalent to the ones used here, but translation is readily accomplished.

[20]Ashby, *Design for a Brain,* pp. 80–99.

Most political scientists portray the homeostatic system with a single feed-back loop.[21]

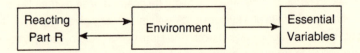

In this system the environment affects the values of the essential variables and also those of the reacting part. When the environment changes, the values of the systemic variables also change to compensate for environmental changes. Note, however, that the structure or field does not change in response to changing environmental conditions. That is, relationships among variables cannot change: only the values of these variables may be affected by the reacting part. It is possible that if the environment changes radically, no change in the values of the systemic variables will be sufficient to allow the essential variables to remain within their critical limits. In this case, the system, so to speak, breaks down; it is no longer in adequate working order. If we postulate a system with a single feedback loop, this is as far as systems analysis can take us.

If we postulate an ultrastable system, or a system with two feedback loops, however, the analysis may continue.[22] Let us suppose again that the first feedback loop has broken down so that in spite of interaction between the reacting part of the system and the environment, the values of the essential variables exceed their critical limits. In this case, the second feedback loop comes into play. Once the values of the essential variables exceed their critical limits, the parameters change. This results in a change in the way in which the reacting part reacts to the environment. In other words, parameter changes result in structural or field changes.

It is possible, of course, that no parameter change will be able to change the way in which the system reacts to the environment in such a way so as to restore the values of the essential variables back within their critical limits. In such a case the system may be said to decay or disintegrate. One would expect, however, that such breakdowns would occur less frequently in the ultrastable system than in the single feedback loop system. Furthermore,

[21]This is similar, for example, to the discussion in Easton, *Framework for Political Analysis*. The diagram used here is from Ashby, *Design for a Brain*, p. 82, by permission of the Estate of W. Ross Ashby and Chapman and Hall.

[22]Note that the ultrastable system is very similar to the system described by Buckley in "Society as a Complex Adaptive System."

since many political systems have survived through structural change, the concept of the ultrastable system would seem more applicable to social and political systems than that of the single feedback loop system.

The Ultrastable System and Johnson's Theory of Revolutions

If we treat the social system as an ultrastable system, Johnson's analysis would probably take on the following form:

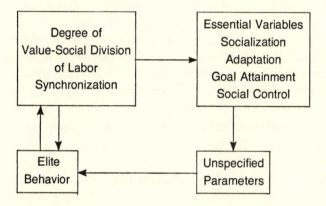

Under the "normal" operation of this system, the elite reacts to changes in the environment to maintain the synchronization between values and the division of labor and, consequently, maintain the values of the essential variables within their critical limits. If this mechanism fails and values become dissynchronized with the social division of labor, the values of the essential variables will be driven beyond their critical limits, and the functional prerequisites of society will not be fulfilled. When this occurs, the elite may introduce conservative change and modify its pattern of behavior so that resynchronization occurs and the essential variables take on, once again, values within their critical limits. If, however, the elite does not initiate conservative change, it will suffer a loss of authority. In this case, either a revolution will occur, or the system will be maintained solely by force. If an accelerator occurs, a revolution will be initiated. This revolution, however, need not necessarily be successful. If it is successful, it will initiate new forms of behavior, corresponding to structural change or change of field, that will achieve a resynchronization between values and the social division of labor. If it is unsuccessful, and the elite still fails to introduce conservative change, the system, presumably, must be maintained, if at all, solely through the use of force.

What should be immediately apparent is that this system remains largely unspecified. In the first place, although the essential variables are specified, their critical limits are not. We do not, then, know how successful socialization has to be, or how much social control is necessary for the system to be considered in adequate working order (or, as Johnson would put it, in equilibrium). The lack of critical limits poses both empirical and theoretical problems. Empirically, it means we have no way of knowing when a given system is or is not in equilibrium. Theoretically, it means that even if we knew the structure or various possible fields of a system, we would still have no way of determining what state of environmental conditions would drive the values of the essential variables beyond their critical limits.

This defect might, perhaps, be overlooked by saying that most social science theories are very imprecise, and in this respect Johnson's theory is no different from others. One might argue that it is "perfectly obvious" that a system will be disequilibrated if, for example, there is "very little" social control. The critical limits, then, might be said to be specified, albeit in a very imprecise manner. This solution might be feasible, although I believe that systems analysis is not likely to prove useful in analyzing problems that cannot be formulated in a more precise manner.

Even if the problem of critical limits were overcome, Johnson's analysis would still suffer from a severe lack of specificity. Virtually all of the components of the system are "black boxes": we do not know how they operate. "Elite behavior," for example, is simply an overall label. It refers to a wide variety of variables and their interrelationships that represent the way in which the elite behaves. The essential variables also are presumably interrelated to some extent, although the theory does not specify these relationships.[23]

Furthermore, the relationships among the components of the system are not very precise. Arrow drawing only indicates some functional relationship among variables. But to say that the value-social division of labor synchronization is some function of, or is affected by, elite behavior is not to say very much. It does not tell us *how* elite behavior affects the degree of synchronization between values and the social division of labor.

The problems caused by this lack of specificity may be illustrated if we consider how an explanation of revolutions would proceed if variables could be precisely measured and the system and environment were completely characterized in terms of structure or fields. Let us assume, in the

---

[23]One would assume, for example, that the extent of social control in a society would be at least partly dependent on the success of socialization.

first place, that we are dealing with a particular system at a particular point in time. This system may be characterized by a description of its state, that is, by the values of its component variables. Now suppose there is some environmental change, and the degree of synchronization between values and the social division of labor changes. If we know the structure, or how the fields are set up, we know how the elite react to this change and how the elite reaction will affect the degree of synchronization between values and the social division of labor. We would also know what affect any changes in the degree of synchronization between values and the social division of labor would have on the values of the essential variables.

If the system and its relationships with the environment were completely specified, then we could trace the effects of any environmental change throughout the system. Furthermore, the effects of the resulting changes in systemic variables on environmental conditions could be traced. If a system were disequilibrated, we could explain why this condition developed by showing how environmental conditions affected systemic variables in such a way that the values of the essential variables were driven beyond their critical limits.

This type of explanation can only be used if the system and its interrelationships with the environment are precisely specified either in terms of a mathematical structure or in the alternative field setup discussed above. If the system is largely composed of "black boxes," there is no way of determining how environmental changes will affect systemic variables. We cannot, then, explain why a value-social division of labor dissynchronization, for example, should result in a situation in which the values of the essential variables exceed their critical limits.

The problem here is fairly similar to the justification problem discussed in conjunction with Gurr's theory. In Gurr's theory, the frustration-agression hypothesis was found to be inadequate for the purposes of explaining postulated relationships among societal-level variables. In Johnson's theory a similar problem arises due to the lack of a structural or field characterization of the system and its relations to the environment. We may postulate that a certain level of value-social division of labor dissynchronization will be correlated with a disequilibrated system. But unless we know the structure or fields of the system, we cannot explain why this level of dissynchronization moves the values of the essential variables outside of their critical limits. In short, the problem again is that although the theory specifies the relevant variables associated with revolution, it does not explain why these variables are associated with revolution.

Thus far we have not discussed the nature of the "parameters" of the ultrastable system. Recall that these parameters govern structural or field changes in systems. To put it another way, if the structural arrangements of a given system are such that, given environmental changes, the system is no longer capable of maintaining the essential variables within their critical limits, it is assumed that the system is capable of structural change. A parameter change, in short, will change the way in which the variables are related to each other. The parameters determine the alternative structure to which the system will move.

Johnson's discussion of structural change is somewhat confusing. To begin with, he argues that the system can maintain the "same" equilibrium if structural change occurs as the result of unintentional evolutionary changes, that is, if the elite does not intend to bring about structural change but unintentionally does so.[24] I am not sure what this means. If Johnson is saying that structural change can occur within the first feedback loop alone (between the elite behavior and the value-social division of labor synchronization), he is wrong. Structural change can simply not arise within a given structure.

Furthermore, the distinction between intentional and unintentional change is somewhat puzzling. There is certainly nothing in the systems analytic perspective to warrant such a distinction. Motivations simply do not enter into systems analysis. Johnson seems to agree with this view when he states:

> There is only one correct way to utilize personality data in conjunction with social systems analysis, and that is through the macro/micro distinction. From the macroscopic perspective of the overall system, the analyst will consider the disequilibrium-induced variations in role performances and the policies of the various conflicting groups in relation to the functioning of the system, regardless of the *motivations* of the actors.[25]

Even if we disregard Johnson's discussion of unintentional change and assume only that structural change might occur as the result of changes initiated by the elite, whether intentional or not, there are still problems with the discussion of structural change. Johnson seems to allow for two kinds of structural change: conservative change initiated by the elite and revolutionary change initiated by a successful revolutionary movement. Revolutionary change, on this account, is only possible if the elite fails to pursue policies of conservative change. So, if a disequilibrated social system is not to be maintained solely through the use of force, the first alternative structural rearrangement would be through conservative change.

The first alternative, however, need not be taken. Johnson does not discuss the conditions under which the elite might be expected to initiate con-

---

[24]Johnson, pp. 55–58.
[25]*Ibid.*, p. 78.

servative change; this is presumably a question decided by their cleverness and free will. But as Kramnick puts it, this "voluntaristic leap of faith" is somewhat hard to take.[26] The theory to this point is quite deterministic. The combination of a disequilibrated social system, elite intrasigence, and an accelerator is supposed to produce a revolution. The behavior of the nonelite who make the revolution, then, is presumably determined by objective social conditions. Why is the behavior of the elite not similarly determined? It is quite possible that Johnson has overemphasized the extent to which the behavior of the "masses" is determined by social conditions.[27] However, he seems to underestimate drastically the extent to which the elite is constrained by these same conditions.

In terms of systems analysis, the failure to specify conditions under which the first structural rearrangement, that is, conservative change, would occur does not present a problem *if* we are willing to view it as a chance phenomenon. In this case, we would simply say that there are two possible changes of structure to which the system might move: one initiated by conservative change and the other through revolutionary change.[28] If conservative change is not adopted, and an accelerator occurs, there will be an attempt at revolutionary change. If conservative change is adopted, revolutionary change becomes impossible unless the system once again becomes disequilibrated. However, there is no way of determining whether or not conservative change will be adopted: in this sense, it is a chance phenomenon. Furthermore, if conservative change is not adopted, the *attempt* to initiate revolutionary change will be made. This attempt may or may not be successful; this, too, is apparently a chance phenomenon. If revolutionary change fails, the system in a sense remains in the same position it was in when it became disequilibrated. Once again, either conservative or revolutionary change becomes possible. If a revolution is successful, and equilibrium is restored, conservative change becomes impossible.

This account, while somewhat convoluted, does not seem to violate principles of systems analysis. But it does, I believe, violate common-sense considerations. There is simply too much chance involved. One might, of course, treat the theory, or at least this part of it, as a first approximation and attempt to develop it further as new evidence is accumulated. I doubt, how-

---

[26]Isaac Kramnick, "Reflections on Revolution: Definition and Explanation in Recent Scholarship," *History and Theory*, XI:1 (1972), p. 47.

[27]This objection has been raised by Lawrence Stone, "Theories of Revolution," *World Politics*, XVIII:2 (January, 1966), p. 166.

[28]It might be more appropriate to view these as sets of structural rearrangements since presumably more than one type of structure could be established through either revolutionary or conservative change.

ever, that Johnson's formulation of the parameters governing structural change can be treated as anything more than a very rough approximation.

The entire analysis here presupposes the assumption that social systems are ultrastable. It might be objected that the criticisms of the theory that have been presented here are unfair since Johnson never states that he is assuming an ultrastable system. I do not, however, believe that Johnson's theory fares any better if other possible systems are assumed. For example, let us suppose he is actually assuming the single feedback loop system that is commonly adopted by social scientists[29]:

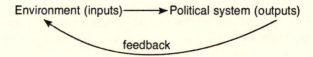

If we adopt this single feedback loop model, we might use the value-social division of labor-synchronization variable as the relevant environmental condition. As the environment changes, the political system reacts to try to maintain the synchronization between values and the social division of labor. If, however, dissynchronization occurs, the system becomes disequilibrated. That is as far as we can go. There is nothing in this model that allows for the analysis of possible structural changes. If we assume a single feedback loop model of the political system, we cannot even develop the bulk of Johnson's theory. The assumption of a single feedback loop system, then, does not allow us to overcome any of the problems encountered when the theory is based on the assumption of a double-feedback, or ultrastable, system. If anything, the analysis is hindered since, on the assumption of the single feedback loop model, much of Johnson's theory is left out.

The problems encountered in Johnson's theory will also not disappear if we omit systems analysis entirely and reformulate Johnson's argument in the more common "causal" form. In this case, the theory basically states that revolutions are caused by a combination of a disequilibrated social system, a loss of authority (or elite intrasigence), and an accelerator. This is simply a list of relevant conditions for revolutions. But, if we omit all considerations of systems analysis, there is no way that the association between these factors and revolutions can be explained. We are left, then, with a theory that lists relevant factors but gives us no reason to believe that these are not merely spurious correlates.

---

[29]Easton, *Framework for Political Analysis*, p. 110.

The assumption of an ultrastable system seems to be the most plausible one to make in interpreting Johnson's theory. But this assumption does not take us far. Without greater specification of the system and its relationships with the environment, there seems to be little way of explaining why a dis-synchronization between values and the social division of labor should lead to a disequilibrated society. Furthermore, Johnson's discussion of the different types of structural change that are possible if a system is disequilibrated seems to rely far too heavily on "chance" or at least unspecified mechanisms.

Testing the Theory

A systems analytic theory of revolutions that was based on a well-specified notion of a social system would be very enlightening. If we could characterize a social system in terms of either its structure or its fields, we would not only have a theory that listed variables relevant to revolutions but also one that could explain the relationships between these variables and revolutions.

One way of developing such a theory would be to use the basic variables suggested by Johnson and to try to develop a more precise characterization of the social system—no easy task. Characterizing a social system in terms of its structure of fields requires much knowledge (or at least speculation). Before proceeding with the task, we should certainly like some assurance that the variables used by Johnson *do* affect revolutions. It would hardly be profitable to expend an enormous effort in characterizing a social system only to find that the relationships we would like to explain through this effort are nonexistent. Before attempting a complicated modification of the theory, then, we would like to be able to test whether the basic relationships postulated hold.

Johnson's theory presents difficult problems of testability. Revolutions, he argues, should be preceded by three conditions: a disequilibrated social system, the failure of the elite to initiate conservative change, and an accelerator. All these conditions are necessary for revolutions to occur; together, they constitute a sufficient condition for revolutions. Neither Johnson nor (as far as I know) anyone else has attempted to test this theory. Instead of evaluating evidence, then, I shall try to examine how this theory might be tested.

There are two ways this theory should be tested. The first would be to examine cases in which a disequilibrated system was combined with the failure of the elite to initiate conservative change and an accelerator. According to Johnson's theory, this combination is sufficient for revolutions. Consequently, in every such case, a revolution should occur.

The second way of testing would be to see if these conditions were necessary; that is, to see whether every revolution has been preceded by a disequilibrated social system, the failure of the elite to implement conservative change, and an accelerator. These tests, of course, could not consist of an examination of all possible cases, but should be based on some "representative" sample of cases, including cases in various historical periods and different parts of the world.

The major obstacle to testing this theory is that there are severe measurement problems. How do we identify revolution? In terms of Johnson's usage, was Allende's regime in Chile a successful revolution or not? This problem is common to many theories of revolution. One way of handling it might be to isolate those instances that virtually all people would consider to be revolutions.[30] This would include such events as the French, Russian, Chinese, and Cuban revolutions as successful instances as well as major unsuccessful attempts such as the Colombian guerrilla war in the 1950s and 60s. A second category could then be established consisting of those events, such as the Chilean "Revolution," that might or might not be considered revolutions. In examining instances of revolutions to test the necessary conditions Johnson uses, only events in the first category—the "sure" revolutions—would be used. However, for sufficiency tests, the theory would only be falsified by a case in which the sufficient conditions obtained but were not followed by an event in either of the above categories. This would give the benefit of the doubt to the theory since it could only be falsified if we were reasonably sure no revolution had occurred.

The other concepts are somewhat more problematical. Johnson's conception of accelerators is dubious. Certainly the third type of accelerator—operations launched by revolutionaries against the armed forces—seems to confuse the causes of the revolution with the revolution itself. The second type of accelerator—the revolutionaries' belief that they can succeed—is virtually impossible to use for testing purposes, as we have no way of knowing what revolutionaries "really" believe. Thus, we have the remaining type of accelerator—factors that directly affect the effectiveness or loyalty of the armed forces. According to Johnson, the most important of these is defeat in war. However, if we just used defeat in war as an accelerator, we would have an inadequate test of the theory, as this would omit considerations of the other types of accelerators.

---

[30]One way of doing this would be to get the judgment of "experts," that is, people who study revolutions.

One possible solution to this problem would be to substitute Smelser's precipitants for Johnson's accelerators in the theory. Johnson's conception of accelerators suffers from both theoretical problems and problems of testability; I do not believe that replacing this concept would be a loss. Smelser's precipitating factors are fairly similar to Johnson's accelerators but seem to overcome some of the problems associated with these.

A precipitating factor, basically, is one that exaggerates the "strain" inherent in a disequilibrated system.[31] Precipitating factors include sudden economic deprivation (such as a sharp rise in inflation), defeat in war, refusal of citizens to acquiesce to a tax imposition, foreign occupation, and the success of revolutionary movements in different countries. This list is probably not complete, but it seems to take us further than we could get if we used Johnson's accelerators. It would not seem unreasonable to use it in a "rough" test of the theory.

The next condition to be investigated concerns the failure of the elite to initiate conservative change. According to Johnson, this results in a loss of authority and is a necessary condition for revolutions. We might test this hypothesis by trying to determine whether a revolution has occurred in spite of the fact that the government (or elite) had initiated widespread reform. If such a case exists, the hypothesis will be falsified. The problem here, of course, is deciding how much reform must be initiated. It is perfectly possible that a government's reform might be "too little and too late" as conservative change. We might again set up three categories: no reform, that is, no conservative change; widespread reform or definite conservative change; and some reform. The latter category would include the "don't know" cases. The hypothesis, then, would only be falsified if a revolution had been preceded by policies included in the widespread reform category. This procedure, of course, is far from ideal, but it will at least allow the theory to be falsified by blatantly contradictory cases.

Finally, we face the problem of finding indicators for the disequilibrated system. Johnson suggests four: increased ideological activity, a rise in the armed forces to total population ratio, an increase in gross and political crime rates, and increased suicide rates.[32] The first three seem dubious as they could equally well be indicative of the onset, or the effects of the onset, of a revolution. The fourth is ingenious. The basic argument for using it is that there are multiple causes of suicide, including unusually adverse personal conditions, cultural and religious factors, and social conditions generating anomie. The first may, for the purposes of social inquiry, be treated as

---

[31] Smelser, *Theory of Collective Behavior,* pp. 352–55.
[32] Johnson, pp. 119–34.

random. The second varies from country to country but is generally fairly constant within a particular country. The third stems basically from Durkheim and is what concerns us. If a system is disequilibrated, the argument goes, anomie may be expected to increase, which will, in turn, produce an increase in the suicide rate. Assuming other causes of variation in the suicide rate may be treated as either constant or as random disturbances; then, a sharp increase in the suicide rate will be highly correlated with system disequilibrium. A "sharp" increase here means an increase that goes beyond the bounds of normal fluctuations in the suicide rate over time. This indicator may not be perfect, but it seems better than the others suggested.[33]

These procedures only allow for a rather rough test of the theory. But fortunately that is all we need. The reason for testing the theory is to see whether the basic relationships hold, so that we may decide if it is worthwhile to modify the theory. We want to know whether Johnson's hypotheses are false, since, if they are, there is little point in trying to explain them through systems analysis. Since this test is in no sense "final" and only serves as a guideline indicating whether or not it seems useful to proceed along lines suggested by Johnson, even a fairly rough test is satisfactory.

Conclusion

It is clear that the first thing to do is that we test the basic relationships postulated by Johnson. If Johnson's hypotheses are not confirmed, there is no reason to construct a characterization of a social system that would allow us to adequately explain these results.

One might, however, question whether such an undertaking should be pursued even if these hypotheses are confirmed. The type of characterization needed to explain why the relationships between these variables should hold is either a mathematical structure of a social system or a description of a social system in terms of its fields and field changes. The latter characterization is undoubtedly easier to achieve. Nevertheless, it amounts to a mammoth undertaking. It requires, in effect, specification of the lines of behavior from all possible origins and under varying environmental conditions. Marx was one of the few social scientists who has attempted this type of characterization of the total social system, and even his work did not include precise specification of all lines of behavior.[34]

---

[33]One problem in using it concerns the availability of data. The World Health Organization, which seems to be the major source for suicide statistics, only has data on suicide rates for selected countries in fairly recent years.

[34]For example, Marx never systematically studied the development of the Asiatic mode of production under colonial influences.

To say that this type of characterization is difficult does not, of course, mean that it should not be attempted. But, it should be emphasized that systems analysis requires much knowledge, or at least speculation, to serve as the basis for adequate theories. Modifying Johnson's theory by specifying fields is not a task that is comparable, say, to modifying Olson's theory by applying a slightly different conception of rationality.

To analyze the structural causes of revolutions, it is probably easier, and may ultimately be more fruitful, to start with a more fully specified theory and attempt to modify particular areas of weakness. This means relying on theories based on assumptions that are far more restrictive than the ones used by Johnson. But this is generally true of political theories: to obtain theories with strong explanatory power, we must usually rely on fairly restrictive assumptions. In the final analysis, Johnson's theory probably fails precisely because the assumptions he uses are too weak to provide the required degree of specificity. Instead of attempting to strengthen Johnson's assumption "from scratch," then, it may be more profitable to simply build on alternative structural theories that start from stronger assumptions.

V

marx's theory of revolutions

Marx, like Johnson, relies on structural assumptions to explain revolutions. However, instead of starting from a basic conception of the nature of all systems, such as that employed in General Systems Theory, Marx restricted his assumptions to political systems or, in many cases, to particular types of political systems. By restricting the scope of his assumptions, Marx was able to employ assumptions that are far stronger than those used by Johnson. And, although some of these assumptions may be questionable, there is no doubt that by relying on these assumptions, Marx was able to develop a theory that is far more specific and intricate than Johnson's.

While complexity and specificity, by themselves, do not guarantee good theories, these attributes are often associated with "interesting" theories. A theory that is specific about relevant variables and their interrelationships and, at the same time, deals with a number of interrelated variables provides a basis for subsequent theory construction. If an analyst finds the original theory inadequate in some area, he can "tinker" with it by modifying one or more variables, reformulating some of the interrelationships among variables, or changing some of the basic assumptions of the theory. A theory that is both complex and well specified may easily serve as the foundation for a school of thought.

This has certainly been true of Marx's theory that has a unique tenacity among theories of revolution. For roughly 100 years, this theory has been modified and reinterpreted. Part of the reason for the continued appeal of Marx's theory is that many twentieth-century revolutions have been made in the name of Marxism. But even if this were not the case, Marx's theory would probably still retain much of its appeal, simply by virtue of its scope and complexity. One may question many aspects of Marxism—to the point, even, of disputing most of its central hypotheses—and still obtain considerable insight from parts of the theory.[1]

At the same time, the complexity of Marxism makes the theory difficult to interpret. For most social theories, interpretation is not a major problem. One may or may not accept the basic assumptions and hypotheses of the theory; nevertheless, the nature or meaning of the theoretical assertions is generally clear. This is not the case with Marxist theory. Marx's writings are voluminous and include everything from political tracts to broad theoretical analyses. As might be expected from such diversity, these works contain numerous assertions that, if not directly contradictory, are often difficult to reconcile with each other. This leaves the analyst considerable room for interpretation. He can—and probably must—emphasize certain statements and disregard others. In some cases, disagreements over the extent to which certain statements should be emphasized are relatively minor and do not affect the core of the theory. In others, these disagreements lead to fundamental differences in interpretation.[2]

Although there are numerous interpretations of Marxism, we may, broadly speaking, identify two major schools of interpretation. The first emphasizes the positivist or scientific character of Marx's thought. It stresses social and economic conditions as the determinants of the nature of social change and tends to view human consciousness largely as a "reflection" of the material conditions of a person's existence. The second major school of interpretation focuses on the Hegelian aspects of Marx's thought. Emphasis is placed on

---

[1]Although the notion of "heuristic value" is currently in justifiable disrepute, the fact that many hypotheses proposed by modern Marxists as well as non-Marxists can be traced back to Marx's writings means that this theory is suggestive in a nontrivial sense.

[2]The possibility of a peaceful transition to socialism offers an example of the type of issue that might be interpreted in different ways but is not of fundamental importance in Marx's theory. The nature and role of dialectical logic, on the other hand, is of crucial importance. In fact, disagreements over this latter issue have led to wholly different conceptions of Marxism.

dialectics and the basic role of human praxis in determining the nature of social change. While these interpretations are not incompatible at every point, they do rest on different philosophical systems and lead to different conceptions of Marxism.[3]

The interpretation I adopt generally relies on the positivist conception of Marxism. This interpretation was adopted as it represents the more common view, and, only with this interpretation does Marxism become at all comparable to the other theories of revolution considered to this point. Nevertheless, at places in which the theory becomes problematical, efforts will be made to consider modifications developed within alternative schools of Marxist thought. In this way, it may be possible to develop a coherent view of Marxism without becoming overly dogmatic about particular issues that have been debated within the Marxist framework.

I will limit my discussion to those elements of Marx's thought that are most directly relevant to his theory of revolutions. This involves an analysis of both the "objective" and the "subjective" conditions that affect revolutions and the interrelationships among these. This analysis, then, focuses on the theory as Marx originally proposed it. While some suggested modifications of this theory will be considered, at places in which they seem helpful, no attempt will be made to consider the full range of Marxist thought on this subject within the past 100 years. This limitation was imposed for practical reasons. An analysis of all of the Marxist theories, hypotheses, and practical guides to revolution, would occupy volumes. To limit this enterprise, it is necessary to consider only those modifications that seem to develop plausible ways of handling gaps encountered in Marx's original theory.

Marx's Theory of Revolutions: An Overview

Marx's theory of revolutions is often summarized by quoting a short but confusing passage from his preface to *A Contribution to the Critique of Political Economy*:[4]

---

[3]For a discussion of the distinction and incompatibility between the two views see Gajo Petrović, "Dialectical Materialism and the Philosophy of Praxis," *Boston Studies in the Philosophy of Science,* IV (Amsterdam: Reidel, 1969), pp. 261–76; and Stanley Moore, "Marx and the Origin of Dialectical Materialism," *Inquiry,* 14:4 (Winter, 1971), pp. 420–29. For a broader discussion of alternative interpretations of Marxism see Helmut Fleischer, *Marxism and History* (New York: Harper & Row, 1973); and Alan Wolfe, "New Directions in the Marxist Theory of the State." Paper presented at the 1973 Annual Meeting of the American Poltical Science Association, New Orleans, September 4–8, 1973.

[4]Karl Marx, *A Contribution to the Critique of Political Economy* in *The Marx-Engels Reader,* ed. by Robert C. Tucker (New York: Norton, 1972), pp. 4–5.

In the social production of their life, men enter into definite relations that are indispensable and independent of their will, relations of production which correspond to a definite stage of development of their material productive forces. The sum total of these relations of production constitutes the economic structure of society, the real foundation, on which rises a legal and political superstructure and to which correspond definite forms of social consciousness. The mode of production of material life conditions the social, political and intellectual life process in general. It is not the consciousness of men that determines their being, but, on the contrary, their social being that determines their consciousness. At a certain stage of their development, the material productive forces of society come in conflict with the existing relations of production, or—what is but a legal expression for the same thing—with the property relations within which they have been at work hitherto. From forms of development of the productive forces these relations turn into their fetters. Then begins an epoch of social revolution. With the change of the economic foundation the entire immense superstructure is more or less rapidly transformed. In considering such transformations a distinction should always be made between the material transformation of the economic conditions of production, which can be determined with the precision of natural science, and the legal, political, religious, aesthetic or philosophic—in short, ideological forms in which men become conscious of this conflict and fight it out. Just as our opinion of an individual is not based on what he thinks of himself, so can we not judge of such a period of transformation by its own consciousness; on the contrary, this consciousness must be explained rather from the contradictions of material life, from the existing conflict between the social productive forces and the relations of production. No social order ever perishes before all the productive forces for which there is room in it have developed; and new, higher relations of production never appear before the material conditions of their existence have matured in the womb of the old society itself. Therefore mankind always sets itself only such tasks as it can solve; since, looking at the matter more closely, it will always be found that the task itself arises only when the material conditions for its solution already exist or are at least in the process of formation.

This passage is confusing in several respects. For instance, no one seems quite sure what the terms "productive forces" and "productive relations" mean. Bober provides a plausible definition of the former.[5] On this account, "productive forces" refers to (1) the way in which labor is organized, including the skills and status of the workers, (2) natural resources, and (3) the state of technology. An improvement in *any* of these would constitute a development of the productive forces of a society. If Bober's account is accepted, relations of production hindering, for example, the development of workers' skills, would constitute fetters on the development of the productive forces. This issue becomes important since there is a tendency among non-Marxists to identify productive forces with technology alone. If "productive forces" simply refers to the level of technology, Marx does indeed be-

---

[5]M. M. Bober, *Karl Marx's Interpretation of History* (New York: Norton, 1965), pp. 6–28.

come the "vulgar economic determinist" he is often accused of being. On the broader definition proposed by Bober, however, this criticism makes little sense.

The relations of production term can also be defined in several ways. Plamenatz generally treats these as referring to property relations.[6] On a more general level, the term may be used to refer to both social and personal relations among those involved in a given system of production.[7] This latter sense seems more in line with Marx's usage that suggests that the term designates such broadly different systems of work and social relations as feudalism, capitalism, and socialism. In this sense, property relations may be seen as the "legal expression" or formal manifestation of basic patterns of stratification and dominance inherent in different forms of society.

At this point, the normative element in Marxist thought comes out strongly. If "relations of production" refer to different systems of social relations, including those of dominance, then it becomes legitimate to conceive of these in normative terms. Some social systems allow for greater possibilities of freedom and the creative development of human faculties than others, and it is in this sense that we may speak of some relations of production as being "higher" than others.

The notion of treating revolutions as movements to social systems that offer greater possibilities for the development of freedom is utterly alien to modern social-science thought. It is currently fashionable to maintain a strict distinction between normative and empirical claims. Furthermore, normative elements are usually banned from scientific studies of politics in an effort to create research that is in some sense "value-free."

Marxist theory is diametrically opposed to this type of separation of fact and value. The theory begins with a conception of human nature as developing throughout the course of history in certain directions. If this development is not to be thwarted, men must progressively create freer societies. The theory aims to explain how and why such development takes place.

To oversimplify, Marx postulates that the relationship between productive forces and relations of production takes the form of a step function, with relations of production appearing as the "dependent" variable. The productive forces, in this scheme, can only develop to a certain point within a given system of productive relations. Once that point is reached, a new and higher system of productive relations must develop if the productive forces are to continue developing. This does not imply, of course, that the productive forces must necessarily continue to develop throughout human history. It

---

[6]John Plamenatz, *Man and Society*, vol. 2 (New York: McGraw-Hill, 1963), pp. 279–83.
[7]This follows the conceptualization adopted by Bober, *Marx's Interpretation of History*, pp. 96–97.

merely asserts that if such development is to occur, that is, if the society is not to stagnate or decay, higher systems of productive relations must periodically replace lower ones. It is this transition between types of relations of production that constitutes a revolution in Marxist theory.

On a general level, the relationship between productive forces and relations of production may be explained by assuming that the structure of certain systems of productive relations generates contradictions. In dynamic terms, this means that the system is not "self-maintaining," that is, it eventually must undergo some type of structural change.[8] The particular contradictions inherent in a given system of relations of production may differ from one society to the next. Nevertheless, all social structures characterized by such contradictions share a common feature: they generate both the conditions for their own downfall and the preconditions for a higher form of society. In other words, if such societies are to continue to develop, the internal contradictions must ultimately be resolved. These contradictions, however, cannot be resolved until the means for their resolution have developed within the society itself. Once these means are fully developed, the old society must perish from its internal contradictions. But, by this point, society will have also developed the material and social conditions for a new form of society characterized by higher relations of production.

At this level, the theory is too abstract to be disputed. It simply asserts that social change is a dialectical process generated by basic contradictions between the productive forces of a given society and the corresponding relations of production. This assertion forms the core of Marxist theory. It cannot, however, be evaluated in isolation from the rest of the theory. To begin to evaluate the utility of conceiving of social change in this manner, we must know what contradictions are generated in the various forms of society, how these lead to the downfall of those societies, and how the preconditions for higher forms of societies are generated.

Unfortunately, Marx paid little attention to precapitalist societies.[9] The bulk of his writing is dedicated to a description of the dialectical process of transformation within capitalist societies. In this sense, Marxism only constitutes a fully developed theory of revolutions for capitalist societies. For this reason,

---

[8]Cf., above pp. 82–5.

[9]It is, of course, possible that Marx was restricting dialectical laws to capitalist nations. This interpretation is favored by George Lichtheim, *Marxism: An Historical and Critical Study* (New York: Praeger, 1965), p. 159, who argues that there is nothing in Marx's writings to suggest he viewed capitalism as somehow arising from the internal contradictions of feudalism. While it is true that Marx's scant writings on feudalism support this interpretation, his more general theoretical works do not. Nevertheless, for our purposes, this issue is not crucial since whether or not Marx thought that the dialectical transformation of feudalism could be used to explain the development of capitalism, it is clear that he never provides such an explanation.

the analysis here will focus only on the theory as it relates to the transition from capitalism to socialism.

To evaluate Marx's theory of revolutions in capitalist societies, we need to examine the nature of capitalist dynamics as it creates conditions that both limit its further growth and give rise to the development of a revolutionary socialist movement. This requires analyzing the theory on two interrelated levels: the first focuses on the mechanisms by which capitalism becomes a fetter on the productive forces, while the second is concerned with the development of a revolutionary consciousness in advanced capitalist societies. Both are aspects of the revolutionary process in Marx's theory, and if the theory is valid, it must be possible to show that both form an interrelated set of developments that are generated by the internal contradictions of capitalism.

The Dynamics of Capitalist Development

Marx's theory traces the dynamics of capitalism as it develops from a manufacturing system to what is now termed monopoly capitalism.[10] Although Marx's categories are very different from those used by most non-Marxist economists, many of his initial assumptions are similar to the familiar "bourgeois" theory assumptions of perfect competition, profit-maximizing entrepreneurs, and so forth. What Marx generally does is start with fairly restrictive assumptions, examine the consequences of these, and then look to see what may happen with a wide variety of other conditions. In analyzing the theory, then, it is important to remember that most of Marx's predictions are not unconditional. Such familiar "laws" as the falling tendency of the rate of profit may be counteracted or even reversed under a variety of conditions that may develop in capitalist societies. This means that tracing the dynamics of capitalist development is a difficult task since it becomes necessary to try to account for the effect of numerous conditions that may develop in particular societies as well as to elaborate the basic trends of capitalism that would hold if the initial restrictive assumptions were met.

Since Marx's theory of capitalist development is most complex, I will present only a bare sketch of those aspects that are directly relevant to the theory of revolutions. To understand Marx's theory of revolutions, we need to know what contradictions are inherent in capitalism, what dynamic tendencies these generate, and what conditions may counteract the development of these tendencies in a given society. This barely begins to cover Marx's

---

[10]For a good summary of Marx's economic thought, see Paul M. Sweezy, *The Theory of Capitalist Development* (New York: Modern Reader Paperback, 1968).

theory of capitalist development, but it should at least give us a clearer idea of what is meant by the Marxist notion that capitalism generates its downfall.

According to Marxist theory, there are numerous contradictions inherent in the structure of capitalism. Since these, in a sense, are all aspects of each other, it is only necessary to discuss some of the major contradictions of capitalism and their effects. Following Bober, we may distinguish three basic contradictions of capitalist society.[11] These are: (1) that production is geared to profit maximization rather than to the satisfaction of human needs and the development of human beings; (2) that although ownership and control of the productive processes are private under capitalism, production itself is increasingly social; and (3) that although production is carried out on a rational and planned basis within the factory, there is no such planning outside individual factories.

As capitalism develops, these contradictions become increasingly manifest. Ultimately, the effects of these contradictions—including the increasing misery of the workers, falling rates of profit, and periodic crises—lead to the system's decay. Although a detailed elaboration of the mechanisms underlying the development of these contradictions would require a heavy dosage of economic theory, it is possible at least to outline the basic rationale for Marx's arguments.

Marx argued that the profit-hungry capitalist faced with a competitive market would constantly be forced to find ways of raising the productivity of the workers. This leads to a rise in what Marx terms the organic composition of capital.[12] Two major results stem from this: as smaller capitalists find it more and more difficult to compete, capital becomes increasingly concentrated in the hands of relatively few individuals; and under the assumption that the rate of surplus value does not rise, the rate of profit will fall.[13]

The falling rate of profit has further consequences of its own. If profit rates do not fall gradually, but decline in spurts, capitalists are likely to react to a fall in the rate of profit by postponing reinvestment of capital. This occurs

---

[11]Bober, *Marx's Interpretation of History*, pp. 206–08. For a somewhat different discussion see Ernest Mandel, *Marxist Economic Theory*, vol. 1 (New York: Modern Reader Paperback, 1970), pp. 132–81.

[12]Roughly speaking, the organic composition of capital, q, is a measure of the amount spent on material, machinery, etc. (known as constant capital c) relative to the amount spent on labor (or variable capital, v). It can be defined as $q = c/c+v$. The discussion here follows Sweezy, *Capitalist Development*.

[13]Surplus value, s, is defined as the difference between (exchange) value and the sum of capital advanced (constant and variable). Roughly speaking, this corresponds to the increment of money gained in the circulation process. If the capitalist starts with some quantity M of money, produces C units of commodities, and then sells these for M', s is equal to M'−M. The rate of surplus value, s', is then defined as $s' = s/v$. The rate of profit, p, is defined as $p = s/(c + v)$. Given these definitions we can, by simple algebraic manipulation, derive the equation $p = s' (1 - q)$. But this means that if q rises and s' does not similarly rise, p must fall.

because the capitalist who is used to a certain rate of profit is not likely to invest capital under less favorable conditions, at least as long as he thinks that conditions may improve in the near future. Failure to reinvest, however, entails an interruption of the process of circulation. If this type of reaction is widespread, the result will be an economic crisis. So, the profit motivation of capitalism, through its dynamic effects on the rate of profit, becomes one of the reasons for capitalist economic crises.

That production, under capitalism, is geared to profit maximization rather than to the satisfaction of human needs will also generate, according to some Marxists, a second source of economic crises: underconsumption. The basic idea is that the capitalists' drive for expansion results in disproportionality between the rate at which consumption grows and the rate at which the means of production are developed. Specifically, consumption will grow at a slower rate than the growth of the means of production. But, this means that the growth in consumption will sooner or later fall behind the growth in the available supply of goods. This, again, may result in the curtailment of production, which interrupts the circulation process and results in an economic crisis.

A final source of capitalist crises stems from the anarchic nature of capitalist production. Because there is no planning, the individual capitalist must estimate the nature of the demand for his good. If he overestimates the demand for his product at a specific price, his rate of profit will fall, and he will curtail subsequent production. If the demand of other producers for commodities that were previously required in his production process does not stimultaneously rise, the result once again will be an interruption of the process of circulation. And, if this occurs on a large enough scale, the result will be economic crisis.

I do not aim to provide anything resembling a full account of Marx's theory of crises.[14] All that I intend is to give some idea of how Marx derives the tendency for economic crises to occur in capitalist societies from his assumptions about the nature of the contradictions within capitalism. If these crises become increasingly severe, even resulting perhaps in chronic depression, it would be quite justifiable to speak of a "breakdown" of capitalism generated by its internal contradictions. But, even granting the basic assumptions of Marxist economic theory, this hypothesis seems dubious. There are numerous conditions that, at various points in the dynamic sequence, can easily counteract the crisis-producing effects of capitalist contradictions. The falling tendency of the rate of profit, for example, can be offset by such diverse factors as speedups and foreign trade. What is even

---

[14]For a discussion of crises, see Sweezy, *Capitalist Development,* pp. 133–236.

more important is that state expenditures can be—and have been—used to regulate the economy and prevent crises. These factors, among others, will drastically slow down, if not completely reverse, the process by which capitalism becomes a nonviable economic system.[15]

If crises do not necessarily guarantee the ultimate decay of capitalism, it is still possible that the contradictions of capitalism generate other effects that are responsible for its downfall. At this point, Marxist theory becomes thorny. The most plausible interpretation seems to be that, although the other major effects of capitalist contradictions do not directly lead to the downfall of the system, they do so indirectly, by creating conditions that offer the possibility of a better form of social relations.

The noncrisis-producing effects of the contradictions of capitalism may be divided into two classes: those that lead to dissatisfaction with capitalism and those that form the preconditions of socialism. The first revolves largely round the issue of the increasing misery of the working class. The second includes both the development of a material basis for socialism as well as the rise of some aspects of cooperative or socialist work relations within capitalism.

The question of the increasing misery of the working class is one of the most controversial issues in Marxist theory. There are three major interpretations of this point. The first is simply that Marx thought the workers would become increasingly impoverished until they were virtually at a subsistence level of existence. The second interpretation is that although the standard of living of the workers may not decline, the gap between workers and capitalists would increase, leading to relative impoverishment. The third interpretation is the most sophisticated, as well as the most plausible. Increasing misery is now treated in more psychological terms.[16] Since Marx argued that human needs are socially determined, this interpretation asserts that the increasing misery of the workers stems from capitalism's ability to create needs it cannot satisfy. For example, the worker, having satisfied his basic material needs, may want an interesting job. But the capitalist wants more profits, and these are most effectively gained when the worker is subject to assembly-line production. Thus, the increasing misery of the working class

---

[15]One can, of course, always argue that the effects of such measures are temporary. It is possible, for example, that if the private sector is to be preserved, state expenditures will become an increasingly inefficient method of regulating crises. For a cogent argument to this effect, see Paul Mattick, *Marx and Keynes: The Limits of the Mixed Economy* (Boston: Extending Horizons Books, 1969).

[16]See Daniel Friedman, "Marx's Perspective on Objective Class Structure," *Polity,* VI:3 (Spring), pp. 318–44, for a discussion of these interpretations. It should be noted that there is little evidence that Marx adhered to the first interpretation. This interpretation is presented here only because it is often ascribed to Marx.

may be due to the fact that, although his wages may rise, the worker develops other needs that are hard to satisfy within capitalism.

At the same time that capitalism creates needs it cannot satisfy, it develops the preconditions for a form of society in which, presumably, these needs can be satisfied. For one thing, under capitalism the productive forces are developed to an unprecendented extent. The introduction of automation means that human labor can be freed from many unpleasant tasks without limiting (and even perhaps enhancing) the ability of the economic system to produce an adequate supply of material goods. This implies that basic human needs for adequate nutrition, housing, and so on, can be satisfied by utilizing only a relatively small fraction of the productive resources of society. The remainder can be geared to the development of human potential, including the possibility of engaging in nonmonotonous creative labor.

Furthermore, there is a sense in which capitalism actually fosters socialist work relations. Marx noted that under capitalism there is a contradiction between the social mode of production and the private method of appropriation. The extreme division of labor that characterizes modern factory production teaches the worker that he is indeed a social being: satisfaction of his goals and desires is heavily dependent on the actions of others, and the satisfaction of others depends on his behavior. If this is true, then the private method of appropriation may appear incongruous. After all, if production is social, why should appropriation be private? The development of joint stock companies may only serve to intensify the feeling that private appropriation of the products of labor belongs to an outdated social system.

The above considerations, however, only indicate that capitalism generates the *possibility* of socialism. The realization of socialism is obviously quite different. Clearly, there can be no socialist revolution unless people decide to make one. The issue then becomes: What in capitalism motivates people—especially workers—to participate in socialist revolutionary movements?[17]

The nature of the "subjective conditions" for socialist revolutions is one of the most complex aspects of Marxist theory. Roughly, mass participation in revolutionary movements is taken to be dependent on the nature of class consciousness. As capitalism develops, the nature of working-class consciousness supposedly develops to a point at which workers both desire a socialist revolution and are willing to pay the costs of participation to achieve it. Since this argument is of crucial importance to the theory of revolutions, I

---

[17]The issue of the success of these movements is generally not treated in Marxist theories. The underlying assumption for this seems to be that if enough people were willing to participate in a revolutionary movement, the capitalists would not have the power to stop them.

will examine it in some detail. To do this, it is necessary to examine Marx's conception of man in capitalist society and the way in which his mode of behavior changes over time. If Marx can show that capitalism generates the subjective, as well as the objective, conditions for socialist revolutions, he will have succeeded in explaining how the conflict between productive forces and relations of production in capitalism leads to socialism. If not, there is an obvious gap in the theory.

Alienation and Class Consciousness

Marx's account of the development of class consciousness is admittedly fragmentary. Although he presented a relatively lucid picture of the nature of man in capitalist society, Marx devoted little time to a systematic exposition of the way in which workers in such societies would develop the types of attitudes that would lead them to participate in socialist revolutionary movements. The account here, then, is necessarily tentative and highly interpretive. However, by combining Marx's account of man in capitalist society with his scattered remarks on participation and the formation of class consciousness, it is at least possible to piece together a reasonably plausible interpretation of Marx's theory of revolutionary participation.

On Marx's conceptualization, all men are characterized by certain needs, or desires, and certain powers, or capabilities, of satisfying these needs.[18] As men increase their capacity to satisfy certain needs, they create other desires that must be satisfied by developing greater capabilities. Thus, there is an interactive relationship between needs and powers, whereby men's desires affect their development of the capacity to satisfy these, which, in turn, creates new environments that lead to new desires. To a certain extent, then, men's desires are social: they depend on the social environment that is created as people satisfy their needs.

In a general sense, this relationship between needs and powers can be extended to cover consciousness as well. That is to say, there is, in Marx's theory, an interactive (or dialectical) relationship between activity and consciousness. Because of his consciousness of his life situation, a person engages in certain activities that, in turn, further mold and shape his consciousness. More precisely, because of their consciousness of the situation they are in, people engage in activities that, together with the activities of others, create certain objective social structures. These "objective" struc-

---

[18]This account of Marx's conception of human nature and man's alienation under capitalism rests heavily on the discussion in Bertell Ollman, *Alienation: Marx's Conception of Man in Capitalist Society* (Cambridge: Cambridge University Press, 1971).

tures serve to change an individual's environment and his consciousness of this environment.[19]

Although "activity" could be extended to cover virtually everything people do, Marx was most concerned with the effects of man's productive activity or work. Productive activity may plausibly be taken to be man's major activity since it is both crucial to his existence and his most time-consuming activity. Thus, the general relationship between activity and consciousness or, what amounts to the same thing, between what men do in life and how they view their life situation may, at least for the purposes of broad social inquiry, be simplified to the relationship between work and consciousness.

Marx attempted to further simplify this relationship to one between *types* of work and categories of consciousness. To do this, he classified work according to its relationships to the means of production, thereby establishing categories of work, or objective classes. Although Marx does not systematically discuss the criteria that are used to differentiate these classes, at least three such criteria are used: (1) ownership versus nonownership of the means of production; (2) control versus lack of control over what is produced; and (3) productive versus nonproductive work.[20] This leaves us with eight potential classes, although in many societies some of these may include no or very few people.

In and of itself, there is nothing wrong with this type of procedure. In fact, if an analysis of social change is to be at all tractable, some simplification must be made. Many people, however, have questioned the usefulness of treating consciousness in terms of classes thus defined. Since the rest of the theory of class consciousness is heavily dependent on this, Marx's categorization of work constitutes one of the most important analytical procedures of the theory. Once this is done, it is possible to analyze the situation of the various classes in capitalist society and to examine how consciousness changes as capitalism develops.

For Marx, alienation is the most important characteristic of work in capitalist society. Under capitalism, the worker becomes alienated from his work, the product of his labor, other men, and the species of man.[21] Work, in Marxist theory, plays a decisive role in the development of human beings. Under capitalism, however, work becomes drudgery, particularly for the proletariat. Instead of developing the worker's capacities, work serves largely to ruin both the worker's body and his mind. This is particularly true of industrial

---

[19]For a more detailed account of this type of learning process, see Peter L. Berger and Thomas Luckmann, *The Social Construction of Reality* (Garden City, N.Y.: Doubleday, 1966).

[20]Friedman, "Marx's Perspective."

[21]The basic source for Marx's theory of alienation is Karl Marx, *The Economic and Philosophic Manuscripts of 1844,* ed. by Dirk J. Struik (New York: International Publishers, 1964).

production, in which assembly-line techniques, hierarchical authority relations, and so on have reduced the worker to a mere cog in the machine. Under these conditions, work becomes only a means for making enough money to satisfy desires or needs for material goods. The actual productive activity, however, leaves the worker unhappy and contributes nothing to the development of his abilities.

Because he is alienated from his productive activity, the worker also becomes alienated from the product of his labor. Again, this is particularly true of the proletariat, who have absolutely no control over the objects they produce. They do not decide what is to be produced, how it is to be produced, or what happens to the products of the labor process. In a sense, they do not even have the satisfaction of knowing what they have produced since assembly-line production allows the worker to see only one small aspect of the production process.

The worker is also alienated from his fellow men. Marx argued that if workers are put in situations in which they are alienated from the product of their labor, their interests must necessarily become opposed to the interests of those who appropriate their products. And, because workers are alienated from capitalists, capitalists are alienated from workers. Furthermore, workers must compete with each other for employment, finding themselves alienated from each other as well as from the capitalists. In short, the capitalist labor process not only estranges man from his work; it also creates conditions under which men are estranged from each other.

Finally, Marx views man as being alienated from his species. This aspect of alienation underlies the others. When Marx talks of species man, he is referring to man's potential for the free and creative development of his human faculties. By creating working conditions in which such development is hindered, capitalism creates the basis of man's alienation.

To an extent, all people in a capitalist society are alienated. To the extent that work is monotonous and, from the point of view of the worker, meaningless, it becomes an alienating activity. Such conditions, however, are most extreme for the proletariat,[22] and it is this class that suffers the most severe form of alienation in capitalist society. At first glance, the most alienated group in society would not seem to be the most likely group to develop a revolutionary consciousness. Nevertheless, Marx argued that it was precisely because of their position in capitalist society that the proletariat would become revolutionary. Although he never discusses this transformation in

---

[22]Using the criteria outlined above, the proletariat would be the class of productive workers who neither own their means of production nor exercise control over the product of their labor. The bulk of this class are industrial workers.

any great detail, scattered writings on the subject may be pieced together to form a plausible interpretation of his argument.

The development of a revolutionary consciousness, according to Marxist theory, is a rather lengthy process that involves the type of interaction between activity and consciousness just described. In other words, workers start with one form of consciousness, engage in certain activities that change the objective conditions under which they live as well as their consciousness of these, and so on. The revolutionary development of the working class, then, is something that emerges gradually as the result of more or less incremental changes in their modes of behavior and consciousness of these.

For our purposes, it is not necessary to trace the course of this development back to the beginnings of capitalism. One of the central tenets of Marx's theory is that the ideas of the ruling class becomes the ruling ideas of every epoch.[23] We may therefore suppose that at some point in the development of capitalism, workers will be imbued with bourgeois consciousness. To evaluate Marx's theory of revolutionary participation, then, we need to know how this bourgeois consciousness becomes transformed into socialist consciousness.

The nature of bourgeois consciousness, in broad outline, is not radically different from the modern notion of economic man. It basically entails the form of self-interested rationality that is frequently assumed by economic theorists. Thus, "bourgeois man" is able to calculate advantages that he evaluates in largely materialistic terms. He is interested in maximizing his own economic position.

If this is the case, it becomes legitimate to ask why the worker does not fall prey to the "free rider" paradox described by Olson. Olson argued that self-interested rational man would not participate in collective action since, if the relevant group were large enough, the additional contribution of an individual member would not affect noticeably the magnitude of the benefits that accrue as the result of collective action, although it would significantly affect the costs that the individual might expect to pay. The rational self-interested worker should not participate in any working-class movement (including a revolution) as long as the goals of such movements are as likely to be realized if he does not participate as they are if he does participate. Since the effects of any individual worker may plausibly be assumed to be negligible, this means that the worker with a bourgeois consciousness should not voluntarily participate in any form of class action.

---

[23]Karl Marx, *The German Ideology* in *The Marx-Engels Reader*, pp. 136–37, and *Manifesto of the Communist Party*, in *The Marx-Engels Reader*, pp. 337–38.

This conclusion poses problems since the idea of socialist consciousness clearly requires some type of collective orientation. If the worker acts on the type of self-interested rationality described above, it is difficult to see how change comes about. It seems as though once the worker becomes imbued with bourgeois consciousness, he will remain in that state indefinitely.

The answer to this problem may perhaps be found in the special conditions of the working class. Although workers, like everyone else in capitalist society, seek personal gain, their work, by the nature of industrial production, must be collective. This means that they come into daily contact with some form of collective action. This does not mean, of course, that they must then voluntarily engage in other forms of collective action. But, it does provide them with this type of experience.

If workers follow Olson's line of reasoning—as they may well do at the outset—they are likely to be stuck with low wages, long hours, and poor working conditions. This, however, goes against their desire to improve their economic position. The workers, then, find themselves in a dilemma: if they act "rationally," they remain poor. The purely self-interested worker may then come to realize that his interests are not best served by purely self-interested action. In this situation, it is possible that workers will change their mode of behavior and engage in collective action designed to improve the economic position of all workers or, at least, all workers in a given locality.

This development, however, would imply some transformation of working-class consciousness, as well as a transformation of the objective conditions with which workers live. If such action were successful, workers would, first of all, find themselves in an improved economic situation. They would also have overcome part of their alienation from their fellow-men. And, by engaging in such activities, they begin to develop a group-oriented perspective. They realize that to fulfill their desires as individuals, they must act on the behalf of others. In short, they begin to develop a form of class consciousness. The very act of engaging in collective action, then, undermines the individualist bourgeois consciousness of the workers.

Even assuming that such developments take place, the worker is still far from the type of socialist consciousness needed for revolutionary participation. There is no reason, at this point, to suppose that workers will either desire a socialist revolution or be willing to make one. If workers seek economic gain and can obtain this under capitalism, why should they risk the costs of revolution?

At this point, the theory becomes sticky. Marx seems to assume that, having overcome part of their alienation, workers will abandon the bourgeois conception of money as the primary object of interest and move, instead, to abolish their alienated conditions of work.[24] But, within the basic Marxist framework, there is little reason to expect this to be the case. The type of motivating force that induces the worker to engage in collective action is simply not generated at this stage.

One possible solution to this problem is to introduce an extraneous element: the revolutionary party. This, of course, is Lenin's famous contribution to Marxist theory and one that has been adopted, with varying degrees of modification, by numerous other Marxist theorists.[25] Lenin's basic argument is that, left to their own devices, workers will develop only a "trade union consciousness." That is, they will form unions to secure economic advantages but will not spontaneously move beyond this stage. Revolutionary consciousness must be instilled in the working class by a vanguard party. This vanguard, with its greater understanding of history, can show the workers where their "true" interests lie and help them move beyond a vague dissatisfaction with the existing state of affairs to a positive program of socialist change.

On theoretical grounds, this view seems somewhat more plausible than the notion that workers spontaneously develop a revolutionary consciousness. But, it still leaves a lot of questions unanswered. For one thing, it does not explain why workers should choose to follow the leadership of the revolutionary party. Why should workers decide that their alienated conditions of work are intolerable and must be replaced by socialist work relations?[26]

One possible answer to this question is that alienation never completely engulfs the worker. However alienated he may be, the worker still retains the sense that something is wrong: that his work is not creative and that it does not contribute to his development as a human being. The revolutionary vanguard may then build on this vague discontent in two interrelated ways. It can explain, in the first place, the broader social significance of forms of work relations, tying such discontent to capitalist social structures. And, in the second place, the vanguard can offer the workers the hope that such situations can be improved. In this way it may instill in workers both the feeling that the existing social and political situation is wrong and the idea that change for the better is possible.

---

[24]See also Bertell Ollman, "Towards Class Consciousness Next Time: Marx and the Working Class," *Politics and Society,* 3:1 (Fall, 1972), pp. 1–24.

[25]V. I. Lenin, "What Is To Be Done?" in *Essential Works of Lenin,* ed. by Henry M. Christman (New York: Bantam Books, 1966), pp. 72–92. For some modifications, see Regis Debray, *Revolution in the Revolution?* (New York: Grove Press, 1967) and Antonio Gramsci, *Selections from the Prison Notebooks,* ed. by Quintin Hoare and Geoffrey Nowell Smith (New York: International Publishers, 1971), pp. 5–23.

[26]This question becomes more pressing in view of the fact that there is no detailed account of the nature of socialist work relations. The worker, then, is being asked to give up economic gains for a highly uncertain "socialist" future.

This analysis, however, seems highly oversimplified. It neglects, for one thing, the fact that workers are socialized to accept such capitalist norms as private property, the role of merit in determining social status, and so on. These norms are not easily discarded. People who have been brought up to believe in them will probably show considerable resistance to abandoning them in favor of socialist ideals.[27] Furthermore, the above account neglects the very complex psychological issues involved in the development and transformation of consciousness.[28] The transition from a personal economic gain orientation to one that focuses on maximizing the creative development of all human beings involves a drastic change in consciousness. It is hard to believe that such change takes place merely because a revolutionary party exists.

This does not mean, of course, that it is fallacious to argue that extraneous elements must be used to explain the development of socialist consciousness among the working class. In fact, on both theoretical and empirical grounds, this view is probably substantially correct. But it is simply not sufficient to postulate that socialist consciousness is somehow "brought" to workers by an outside agent. We need to know what types of interactions between workers and revolutionaries must take place if the appropriate change in consciousness is to occur.

The Marxist theory of the development of class consciousness, in short, can only explain the changing nature of working-class consciousness to a certain point. It offers a detailed and fairly plausible account of the development of "trade union consciousness." Beyond this, only the bare outlines of the theory have been drawn. To adequately explain the formation of a revolutionary working class, the various additional elements, including a revolutionary vanguard, and the effects of socialization need to be integrated together.[29] Until this is done, the theory of class consciousness must be deemed incomplete.

The Possibility of a Socialist Revolution

Evaluating the empirical support for Marx's theory is a difficult task. Non-Marxists point to the fact that there have been no socialist revolutions in

---

[27]Some Marxists have done considerable work in this and related areas. For a relatively readable example see Herbert Marcuse, *One-Dimensional Man* (Boston: Beacon Press, 1964).

[28]The integration of Marxism and psychoanalysis is a fairly recent phenomenon that has been developed largely under the influence of the Frankfurt school. For a discussion of such attempts, see Bruce Brown, *Marx, Freud, and the Critique of Everyday Life: Toward a Permanent Cultural Revolution* (New York: Monthly Review Press, 1973).

[29]Although Marxists have been doing considerable work in this area, I have seen no study that manages to successfully accomplish this task.

advanced capitalist societies as conclusive refutation of the theory. As a bonus, they sometimes also point out that the only socialist revolutions that have occurred have taken place in underdeveloped countries. This latter point, it should be noted, is not especially relevant since Marx never analyzed such societies in any depth and made few predictions concerning their development.[30]

However, Marxists can point to developments in capitalist systems, particularly the concentration of capital and the growth of monopolies, that support the theory. Furthermore, there are some scattered studies that tend to support particular hypotheses suggested by Marx's analysis.[31]

All this, however, does not provide much help. That there has been no socialist revolution in advanced capitalist countries does not mean that there will be none, even if Marx himself tended to think that revolutions were imminent in Europe 100 years ago. This simply means that his timetable was wrong, and, anyway, there is little in Marx's analysis to support such a timetable. The absence of socialist revolutions, then, does not automatically disconfirm the theory. At the same time, this fact hardly serves to make the theory any more plausible.

Pointing to the growth of monopolies and similar phenomena will likewise not take us very far. It is entirely possible that although some aspects of Marx's analysis of capitalist development were correct, his analysis of revolutionary change was not. In evaluating his theory of revolutions, it is not sufficient to note that some developments predicted by Marx have come true. We also need to know whether these developments will have the predicted effects on revolutionary change.

These examples illustrate some of the problems involved in using empirical evidence to test Marx's theory. One of these—perhaps the major one—is that although Marxism is a dynamic theory, time factors are not precisely specified. Thus, we never know how long particular processes are supposed to take. If some predicted effect fails to materialize, then, it is never clear whether this means that the theory is inadequate or simply that insufficient time has elapsed.

A second problem of testability stems from the conditional nature of Marx's

---

[30]Marx's scattered writings on noncapitalist countries are mainly journalistic and not terribly profound. See, for example, Karl Marx, *On Colonialism and Modernization*, ed. by Shlomo Avineri (New York: Doubleday, 1969).

[31]See, for example, Mark Abrahamson, *et al.*, "The Self or the Collectivity: Simulation of a Marxian Hypothesis," *Social Forces*, 47:3 (March, 1969), pp. 299–305; Alejandro Portes, "On the Interpretation of Class Consciousness," *American Journal of Sociology*, 77:2 (September, 1971), pp. 228–44; Adam Przeworski and Glaucio A. D. Soares, "Theories in Search of a Curve: A Contextual Interpretation of Left Vote," *The American Political Science Review*, LXV:1 (March, 1971), pp. 51–68.

predictions. In many cases, Marx derives his predictions from simplified assumptions that may not be met in particular historical situations.[32] While Marx notes historical conditions that may offset or reverse the general trends predicted by the theory, he often does not analyze the effects of these on the potential for revolutionary change in a society. For example, imperialism may serve to decrease the organic composition of capital, thereby diminishing or possibly even reversing the falling tendency of the rate of profit and its consequent effects. This means that crises may not be as severe in advanced capitalist societies as Marx originally predicted. However, it is not clear what, if any, effect this has on prospects for revolutions in such societies.

Given these problems, it seems that the only reasonable way to use empirical evidence in evaluating Marx' theory is to see whether the general developments predicted by the theory have occurred in particular capitalist societies and, if not, whether the absence of such developments seems crucial in evaluating prospects for revolutionary change. We cannot simply assume that predictions that have thus far failed to materialize must come true in the future. On the other hand, we cannot use the failure of some predictions as a disconfirming instance without analyzing whether or not this failure seems to be merely a matter of time or a consequence of the fact that particular historical conditions offset the hypothesized effect.

This means that to evaluate the empirical support for Marx's theory, we must rely on additional assumptions that go beyond the scope of Marxism. But, this is true of all theories: in general, in order to test a theory, auxiliary assumptions concerning measurement, categorization, and even effects of particular conditions, must be made. That the type of assumptions needed to test Marxist theories are often more controversial than the ones used to test other social theories only means that any conclusions made on the basis of these tests must be even more tentative than is usually the case.

The basic assumptions that I will use in evaluating the empirical adequacy of Marxism are: (1) people tend to change their basic values slowly, so that we can estimate probable changes in the basic values held by different groups in a society by examining how such values have changed in the past; and (2) one way of estimating the likelihood of change generated by a given social cleavage is to see whether other cross-cutting cleavages seem strong enough to undermine the antagonisms generated by the particular cleavage in question. Both of these assumptions are geared to overcoming the basic time problems posed by Marx's theory. The first means that we can determine whether class consciousness is likely to develop in the predicted fashion

---

[32]See above, p. 102.

in the relatively near future by noting whether it has developed along predicted lines in the past. A second check—and this is particularly useful in
cases in which trends are not very clear—is to see whether class conflict or,
at any rate, class identification is strong enough to generate further increases in class consciousness. In situations in which other cleavages
divide classes in highly salient ways, it seems reasonable to suppose that
the development of class consciousness along Marxist lines will be hindered.
These assumptions are not the only ones that could be used, but they seem
relatively reasonable and probably adequate for the purposes here.

Although an empirical test of this nature is a mammoth task that goes well
beyond the scope of this essay, it is possible to gain some insight into this
question by examining broad historical trends in at least one advanced
capitalist country: the United States. If the above assumptions are accepted,
I would argue that there is little to suggest the development of a socialist
revolution along lines predicted by Marx in this country. That is, many of the
developments predicted by Marx have failed to materialize, and those that
have occurred do not seem likely to generate their predicted effects, at least
in the relatively near future.

For example, U.S. capitalism has been far more successful at regulating
crises than Marx foresaw. In his analysis of capitalist crises, Marx generally
assumed that the state would not play an active role in regulating the
economy. The development and acceptance of Keynesian economics, however, has led the U.S. government to play an increasingly crucial role in
economic regulation. It is possible, of couse, that such regulation will become increasingly inefficient. Certainly, the country is still beset by severe
economic problems, including both inflation and recession. But this does not
mean that such problems must ultimately become so severe that there will
be an economic breakdown. Furthermore, even if Keynesian techniques fail
to prevent severe economic crises in the future, it is quite possible that
capitalism will develop alternative mechanisms for coping with such problems. U.S. capitalism has survived severe economic crises before and may
well do so again. There is little indication, in short, that the contradictions of
capitalism will result in the collapse of U.S. capitalism as a viable economic
system.

In addition to crises, Marx argued that the contradictions of capitalism
would generate the preconditions for socialism and the increasing misery of
the working class. In a material sense, it is probably quite true to say that
U.S. capitalism has generated the basis for socialism. There is an extensive
factory system, the economy is capable of generating material abundance,
and modern technology has developed numerous labor-saving devices that
might be used to free workers from some of the more tedious tasks involved

in the production process. All this makes it easier to construct a viable socialist society. But this only means that capitalism has developed conditions that make socialism possible. In and of themselves, there is no reason why such conditions necessitate a socialist revolution or even make it likely that one will occur. Although Marx was probably correct in arguing that capitalism generates the preconditions for socialism, then, we cannot use this argument to infer anything about the likelihood of a socialist revolution.

If "increasing misery" is interpreted in psychological terms,[33] there is some evidence that the hypothesis is true.[34] A recent study indicates that many workers in this country are dissatisfied with their jobs and feel that they are being treated like machines.[35] Reports of factory sabotage and the abuse of drugs and alcohol by workers in factories only confirm the view that there are probably many workers who share Marx's view that work under capitalism is only a means for making money: it contributes nothing to the development of the workers themselves.

This result, however, only indicates that many workers probably are alienated in Marx's sense of the term. It does not demonstrate that workers will extend feelings of job dissatisfaction to dissatisfaction with capitalism. In other words, workers may not translate alienation into revolutionary consciousness. So an acceptance of Marx's hypotheses concerning the development of alienation in capitalism does not imply that socialist revolutions will occur in advanced capitalist societies.

In examining Marx's theory of alienation, I argued that while there were plausible theoretical reasons for supposing that workers would develop some form of "trade union consciousness," there was little in Marx's theory to support the argument that trade-union co..sciousness would develop into a revolutionary socialist consciousness. Historical trends in the U.S. seeem to bear out this contention. While workers have fought to establish trade unions and secure economic gains, they have not, in the main, become socialists.

Although the lack of revolutionary class consciousness may be due simply to working-class immaturity or to the absence of an organized revolutionary party, at this stage there is no indication that workers are likely to develop a revolutionary class consciousness in the foreseeable future. Certainly, there is no indication that workers are leaning toward socialism on an increasing

---

[33]See above, pp. 105–6.

[34]If it is interpreted in economic terms, the hypothesis is probably false since available evidence indicates that the economic position of workers, in absolute terms, has improved over time. However, it may still be true that the *relative* share of the social product going to labor has not increased over time and, consequently, that dissatisfaction will be induced by unfavorable social comparisons.

[35]Studs Terkel, *Working* (New York: Pantheon Books, 1974).

scale. If anything, what political dissatisfaction exists among U.S. workers seems more geared to reactionary than revolutionary channels. George Wallace, after all, hardly portrays the image of a socialist leader.

Furthermore, the political conflict generated by class divisions does not seem strong enough to produce the kind of class struggle that Marx predicted would develop in advanced capitalist societies. If class conflict were the major social conflict experienced by most people, and if this conflict were becoming politicized, there would be some reason for supposing that class consciousness could develop along revolutionary lines. But, in the U.S. there are other social conflicts that seem to undermine working-class unity on both economic and political issues. Race cleavages undoubtedly produce the strongest conflict of this type, but there are indications that other issues, such as sex discrimination, are likely to divide the working class to an even greater extent. Until these types of issues are settled, it seems highly unlikely that the U.S. will experience the development of a politically united, revolutionary working-class movement.

On empirical as well as theoretical grounds, then, there is little reason to expect job dissatisfaction to develop into revolutionary consciousness. Workers may well choose to push for greater material benefits and accept alienating work as one of the necessary evils of life. As long as workers feel that their children have a chance of "making it" in the middle-class world, and as long as a variety of issues divide the working class, this prospect seems far more likely than the revolutionary alternative predicted by Marx.

These predictions, of course, assume that future changes in class consciousness can be projected from past trends. This was one of the auxiliary assumptions adopted at the outset, and it is a crucial one. Many Marxists, however, would object to this assumption on the grounds that vast structural changes might radically change the nature of class consciousness, both in the U.S. and in other advanced capitalist countries, in the not too distant future.

The most important change of this kind would be the demise of imperialism. According to some Marxists, advanced capitalist countries have managed to stave off the economic effects of capitalist contradictions for a limited period of time by becoming imperialist.[36] Furthermore, imperialism has allowed modern capitalists to amass superprofits that can be used, in

---

[36]The most famous version of the Marxist theory of imperialism is V. I. Lenin, *Imperialism: The Highest Stage of Capitalism* (New York: International Publishers, 1939). Lenin's views have been developed and refined in numerous ways. See, for example, Mandel, *Marxist Economic Theory*, vol. 2, pp. 441–547 and Paul A. Baran and Paul M. Sweezy, *Monopoly Capitalism* (Middlesex, England: Penguin Books, 1966).

part, to "buy off" large segments of the working class. Imperialism, in short, has delayed the revolutionary transformation of capitalist societies by temporarily blocking the development of both the objective and the subjective conditions for a socialist revolution. Because of imperialism, capitalist economies can still operate more or less efficiently, and workers in capitalist countries can reap the material advantages of foreign exploitation. Thus, workers fail to become revolutionary, and capitalism is preserved.

Those who adhere to the theory of imperialism would argue that this state of affairs cannot last forever. Imperialism generates its own contradictions, and these, in turn, lead to the downfall of imperialism. The mechanisms underlying this process are, unfortunately, too complex to be discussed here. However, for purposes here, we may simply treat theories of imperialism as a complex hypothesis that can be used to explain why revolutions in capitalist countries have not materialized.

The question then become whether this hypothesis can also be used to save the basic thrust of Marx's theory, that is, whether it satisfactorily explains how imperialism, as the most advanced stage of capitalism, generates conditions for a mass socialist movement. Here I would argue that theories of imperialism are deficient. Modern Marxists have proposed elaborate theories about the way in which imperialism operates and the conditions that lead to the demise of imperialism. They have also tied imperialism to an explanation of U.S. foreign policy. They have not, however, analyzed how the fall of imperialism will lead workers in capitalist countries to form a revolutionary socialist movement.[37] Since, for our purposes, this gap in theories of imperialism is crucial, it is important to analyze this issue in some detail.

Let us suppose, for the sake of argument, that these theories of imperialism correctly predict the downfall of imperialism. What then? The most direct effects for the imperialist countries, in general, and the U.S., in particular, would be economic. If theories of imperialism are correct, the U.S. would no longer be able to amass superprofits from developing areas. This, in turn, assuming again that such theories are correct, would lead to a decrease in the standard of living of the working class.

At this point, Marxist theories of imperialism predict changes in class consciousness that will culminate in a mass socialist revolutionary movement. These changes, however, are not explained within theories of imperialism. It is simply assumed that with the demise of imperialism, the

---

[37]This point is argued quite forcefully in Bernard S. Morris *Imperialism and Revolution* (Bloomington: Indiana University Press, 1973).

mechanisms of class consciousness development postulated by Marx's theory will begin to operate.[38] Imperialism, then, serves only to delay the revolutionary mechanisms described by Marx.

If Marx's theory of the development of class consciousness rested on the assumption of a decreasing standard of living, it might be plausible to assume that if the demise of imperialism resulted in a decreased standard of living, class consciousness would begin to develop along lines predicted by Marx. But Marx's theory of the development of class consciousness does not assume a decreased standard of living.[39] In fact, there is no clear association in Marx's writings between the development of capitalism and the standard of living of the working class, on the one hand, or between the standard of living of the working class and the development of a revolutionary working class consciousness, on the other.[40] Thus, there is no reason, within Marx's theory, to assume that a change in the workers' standard of living will have any effect on the development of the class consciousness of workers.

This means, though, that there is no basis in Marx's theory for supposing that the end of imperialism will result in a change in working class consciousness along lines predicted by Marx. The burden of linking imperialism with revolution must therefore fall on theories of imperialism. If such theories are used to modify Marx's theory of revolutions, they must include an explanation of how imperialism generates conditions for a socialist revolution. Within the framework set by Marx's assumptions, such an explanation would have to consist of an analysis of the way in which contradictions inherent in imperialism would generate both the objective and the subjective conditions for a socialist revolution in advanced capitalist societies. As they presently stand, none of the Marxist theories of imperialism accomplish this task. We

---

[38]Some of these theories predict revolutionary movements in underdeveloped countries as an intermediary stage between imperialism and socialism in developed countries. However, such theories do not explain how, if at all, revolutions in underdeveloped countries generate conditions for revolutions in developed countries.

[39]See above, pp. 107–13.

[40]Marx predicted that the contradictions of capitalism would lead to the increasing misery of the working class. The term increasing misery, however, may be interpreted in a variety of ways, (see above, pp. 105–6), and does not necessarily imply a decreased standard of living. Furthermore, if "increasing misery" is interpreted in strictly economic terms, i.e., as a decreased standard of living, this condition is not linked to the formation of a revolutionary working class consciousness. Class consciousness, in Marx's theory, develops in the process of the class struggle, that is, it emerges gradually as workers unite against capitalists to gain material, political, and social benefits. There is no reason in Marx's theory for supposing that decreased economic benefits would further the development of class consciousness. In fact, at one point Marx even made the contrary argument, claiming that "once the worker's material situation has become better, he can consecrate himself to the education of his children; his wife and children do not need to go to the factory, he himself can cultivate his mind more, look after his body better, and he becomes socialist without noticing it." Speech to a delegation of German trade unionists (1869), in David McLellan, *The Thought of Karl Marx* (London: Macmillan, 1971), pp. 175–6.

have no reason to believe, then, that any discontent that may stem from the demise of imperialism will be politicized or, if it is, that it will be politicized along revolutionary socialist lines. Theories of imperialism, in short, do not provide us with a theory of revolutions. Until these theories are modified to include an explanation of revolution, they cannot serve as useful modifications of Marx's theory of revolutions.

I argue, then, that Marxist theories of imperialism do not change these conclusions. Marx correctly predicted that capitalism would generate both a material basis for socialism and alienation among the working class. Modern theories of imperialism may be correct in predicting the collapse of imperialism, but this remains to be seen. But Marx was not correct in predicting the development of a revolutionary working class consciousness, and theories of imperialism give us no reason to believe that this prediction will come true in the near future. Available evidence indicates that U.S. workers are not socialist, and show no signs of forming a mass revolutionary movement.

Conclusion

Marxism is probably the most elusive theory of revolutions considered here. With the other theories, it is relatively easy to determine where the theory fails. With Marxism, such evaluation is more difficult.

Part of the problem may be that, in terms of the criteria for evaluation as used here, Marx is neither wholly successful nor wholly unsuccessful in any area. While Marx specifies factors relevant to revolutions, in some cases it is not clear how these factors are supposed to affect the likelihood of revolutions. Crises are the most notable example of this. Some of Marx's writings suggest that crises are related to the economic viability of capitalism, which, in turn, is related to the probability of the occurrence of a socialist revolution,[40] but other writings suggest a variety of factors that may inhibit the severity of capitalist crises.[41] If Marx's theory is interpreted to mean that economic crises are a necessary condition for socialist revolutions, or even that such crises increase the probability of socialist revolutions, then factors that tend to inhibit crises must assume great theoretical importance. However, if crises affect the likelihood of socialist revolutions only in a marginal way, then such factors may perhaps be ignored in a discussion of revolu-

---

[40]See, for example, *A Contribution to the Critique of Political Economy* and *Manifesto of the Communist Party*.
[41]See above, pp. 104–5.

tions. In any case, Marx's writings do not clearly indicate the way in which severe crises are related to revolutions.

Likewise, Marx's theoretical justifications for the inclusion of relevant factors are excellent in some cases and unsatisfactory in others. Generally, Marx gives elaborate theoretical reasons for his hypotheses. In some cases, however, these justifications are not totally adequate. Marx's discussion of the development of class consciousness is particularly troublesome in this respect. While Marx can provide plausible theoretical arguments for the development of "trade union consciousness" among workers in capitalist states, little in Marx's theory explains how or why this type of consciousness will develop into a revolutionary class consciousness.

Finally, Marx's empirical support is ambiguous. While some developments predicted by Marx have occurred, others have not. In this area as well, the development of class consciousness seems to be the crucial pitfall. Although workers have, by and large, developed a trade-union consciousness, and there is evidence that many workers experience the type of alienation that Marx associated with capitalism, there is no indication that workers are in the process of developing a revolutionary class consciousness.

Since the development of class consciousness is the major aspect of Marx's theory of revolutions that suffers from both theoretical and empirical problems, it is not surprising that many modern Marxists have focused attention on this area. However, the results of this effort do not seem conclusive. The major achievement in this area has been to show how ideology can inhibit the development of class consciousness. As I see it, there is no plausible explanation of the formation of revolutionary consciousness. This type of account would constitute a crucial part of a Marxist theory of revolutions.

The work that has already been done in this area suggests that the problem of changing consciousness is highly complex and involves consideration of a number of different factors. The effects of socialization and the role of a revolutionary party in overcoming these effects seem to be particularly crucial areas of investigation. It is not enough to simply argue that a socialist revolution is in the "true" interest of the workers. We must also know how they come to see it as such, in spite of the fact that they have been brought up in a society in which the predominant values are often quite different from those espoused by socialists. This involves integrating both psychological and organization theories into a basic Marxist framework.

This task would be difficult enough. Unfortunately, however, there are a variety of other factors that complicate this issue further. The role of cross-cutting cleavages has already been considered in this respect. Under particular historical circumstances, social cleavages such as race, religion, nationality, or ethnicity may be as important as class divisions in explaining changing social consciousness. This means that the class basis of Marxist theories probably needs to be modified, at least to the extent that the effects of other major cleavages in a society can be taken into account.

Finally, a variety of issues that have not been discussed may need further elaboration within the Marxist framework. The role of the state in fomenting or preventing social change is a case in point. It is entirely possible that an enlightened bourgeoisie can grant premature concessions to other groups that actually hinder the development of revolutionary consciousness. Government-sponsored trade unions provide one example of this phenomenon. In elaborating a theory of consciousness, such contingencies may have important effects.

The need to consider a variety of factors, such as the ones just outlined, means that the construction of an adequate theory of the development of class consciousness is likely to be a long, arduous task. Nevertheless, it does not seem to be beyond the realm of possibility. Marxism is sufficiently well developed to provide a firm basis for this type of modification. A Marxist theory revised along lines suggested here may ultimately prove to be the closest thing available to an adequate theory of revolutions.

VI
CONCLUDING remarks

The study of revolutions sometimes appears to be difficult enough to drive an analyst to despair. Certainly the issues raised in this field are enormously complex. It is hard enough to deal with questions of ordinary political partici-pation. When one considers why people would risk their lives for a political cause, the problems of participation studies are obviously magnified, and participation is only one aspect of the study of revolutions. It is one thing to know why people join revolutionary movements and quite another to deter-mine the conditions under which such movements are likely to succeed.

While the complexities of these issues pose severe problems for any analysis of the causes of revolutions, an examination of existing theories indicates that the situation is far from hopeless. To be sure, none of the theories that have been examined satisfies all of the criteria for theoretical adequacy. However, in terms of these criteria, none is a total failure. Moreover, that there is no single area in which these theories consistently fail suggests that constructing a theory of revolutions that would satisfy all of the imposed criteria may not be impossible.

What does seem clear is that it is very difficult to develop a theory that is both formally well constructed and empirically adequate. Olson's theory is probably the best example of this. Structurally, the theory is excellent. It specifies relevant variables and, through the use of rationality assumptions, explains why these variables are relevant. The only problem with the theoretical development is the lack of specification of the kinds of psychological benefits that might accrue to an individual as a result of collective action. However, since the theory covers all collective action, this problem is not severe. One cannot expect a broad theory to pinpoint all of the specific aspects of particular issues. In terms of his theoretical development, Olson is outstanding.

The main problem with this theory lies in the area of empirical adequacy. If psychological gratification is included as a kind of selective incentive, the theory becomes untestable. If this type of benefit is ruled out, the theory is "falsified" by all mass revolutions under fairly standard assumptions. While mass revolutions are undoubtedly rare events, they do occur and, at least for studies of revolution, are important phenomena. Thus, a theory of revolutions that cannot adequately explain mass revolutions has severe problems.

Problems with the other theories, however, are no less serious. Gurr's theory poses problems that are almost the reverse of the problems of rational-choice theories. In a certain sense, Gurr's theory does not suffer on empirical grounds. At any rate, Gurr presents a wealth of evidence indicating that his predicted associations do, in fact, occur. But, given theoretical problems, this evidence becomes difficult to interpret. The main problem with Gurr's theory is that it is not well developed theoretically. Gurr only specifies relevant variables and indicates, in a fairly vague fashion, how these are related to political violence. He does not specify exact relationships, nor does he justify inclusion of variables by explaining why the posited relationships should obtain.

This type of theoretical problem becomes serious for two reasons. In the first place, it means that Gurr's explanation of political violence becomes vague. The theory merely tells us that certain factors are associated with political violence. It does not specify, in any exact way, how these factors are associated with violence, nor does it indicate why these factors are associated with violence. This means that even if all of the hypothesized relationships are true, we do not know very much about the causes of political violence. This is bad enough. But the theoretical problems lead to a second difficulty: in the absence of a well-developed theory, it is almost impossible to judge the validity of the evidence. Since Gurr does not justify inclusion of variables, we cannot determine whether his reported associations reflect genuine "causal" relationships or are merely spurious correlations. Furthermore, since the exact form of the hypothesized relationships is not specified, it is extremely difficult to judge whether or not the statistical tests used to assess the evidence are likely to yield significantly biased results. In short, because of formal problems of theory construction, it becomes difficult to interpret the kind of evidence presented by Gurr.

I do not wish to argue here that, without theories, facts become meaningless. I do think, though, that theories structure our realities to some extent; that to interpret facts presented as evidence for or against a given theory, we must first have a theory that is reasonably well developed. I would even argue that if our goal is the construction of a general theory of revolutions, our first priority should be the construction of a formally well developed theory. This does not mean, of course, that historical evidence can or should be ignored. Theories are designed to explain events in the "real world," and there is no way of judging the extent to which any theory succeeds in this respect without considering empirical evidence. The point here is simply that facts are no substitute for a well-developed theory.

Johnson's theory provides the best illustration of this issue. In formal terms, the theory is poorly developed. In the first place, major variables are not precisely specified. "Elite behavior," for example, seems to be more a catchall phrase for a wide variety of behavior than a specific variable that is, even in principle, measurable. Furthermore, although Johnson uses systems-theory assumptions to explain how relevant variables can interact in such a way that a revolution occurs, he does not rely on assumptions that are strong enough to accomplish this task. What emerges, then, is a theory that is inadequate both in terms of specification of relevant variables and in terms of the justification provided for these.

In and of itself, Johnson's theory is untestable. To test the theory, an analyst would have to rely on other theories, such as theories of the social implications of suicide, in addition to more standard hypotheses about measurement. This, perhaps, is not a major problem. However, even if such an effort were entirely successful, it would hardly generate an adequate theory of revolutions. In fact, it would only indicate whether some of the posited relationships appeared to be empirically significant. Explaining how and why these relationships work remains a theoretical task and, as the theory now stands, it is a mammoth one. Furthermore, it is entirely possible that a more fully developed structural-functional theory of revolutions would have to be tested by entirely different kinds of evidence. Empirical investigation, then, cannot replace theory construction, although it may—and probably should—aid the task of formulating better theories.

The necessity for coordinating empirical and theoretical work, as well as the difficulty of such endeavors, also shows up in Marx's theory of revolutions. In terms of the criteria used here, this theory is the most difficult to evaluate. With the other theories, it is relatively easy to determine which criteria are satisfied and which are not. Marx's theory is more complicated in this respect since all criteria are satisfied to some extent, but none is satisfied completely. What is interesting here, though, is that there appear to be very definite links between theoretical gaps and problems with the empirical adequacy of the theory.

The most important of these links occurs in the area of participation in revolutionary movements. Marx argues that as capitalist societies develop, workers become increasingly class conscious and eventually form a revolutionary movement that is designed to overthrow capitalism. I have argued that, at least on one interpretation of Marx, it is possible to explain how workers in an alienated state of existence could move from a form of bourgeois consciousness to a "trade union" consciousness. However, Marx does not develop this argument to explain how the same dynamics propel workers to develop the kind of revolutionary consciousness that is a necessary condition for a working-class revolution. Empirically, there is evidence indicating that workers in capitalist countries are alienated, in the Marxist sense of the word, and that workers in capitalist countries develop a trade-union consciousness. There is, however, no indication that workers in capitalist countries are developing a revolutionary socialist consciousness. The part of the theory that receives no empirical corroboration is the same part that is not well developed theoretically.

A survey of these theories indicates, then, that none of the criteria that have been imposed on theories is too strict, in the sense that the criterion cannot be satisfied by any theory of revolutions. However, these criteria are extremely difficult to satisfy—taken simultaneously. This makes it difficult to evaluate the contributions these theories have made and the types of subsequent investigation needed to develop better theories. If we could isolate particular aspects of theories of revolution that satisfy both theoretical and empirical adequacy requirements, we might be able to pinpoint precise areas that need further investigation. Unfortunately, this procedure is generally impossible to follow for most of the theories that have been considered here. However, we can compare theories in broad areas to at least determine which hypotheses seem likely to yield fruitful results.

In terms of broad categories, the two aspects of revolutions that have been dealt with extensively are: (1) participation in revolutionary movements, and (2) success of revolutionary movements in gaining political power. The participation issue is considered by both Olson and Marx. Furthermore, if Gurr's theory is treated on the level of individuals, it also provides an explanation of individual participation in revolutionary movements. This means that we have two broadly divergent participation hypotheses to consider: (1) an individual participates in a revolutionary movement as a result of a rational choice, or (2) an individual participates in a revolutionary movement because of certain psychological mechanisms that may or may not conform to a rational decision-making process. The first hypothesis is developed, in different ways, by both Olson and Marx. The second is presented by Gurr.

First, consider the rationality hypothesis. As Olson uses the term, a rational individual is one who chooses among alternative courses of action by comparing the expected costs and benefits accruing from each and then engages in the particular course of action that has the highest net benefit. If this conception of rationality is accepted, Olson's basic argument cannot be refuted. Since the benefits (or costs) of a revolution are available to everyone, the basic difference in net benefits from alternative courses of action stems from possible selective incentives (including private "costs") that may be tied to participation. The average individual—one who does not expect that his actions will significantly affect the probability that a revolution will be successful—should not rationally participate in a revolutionary movement simply because he favors a revolutionary society.[1] He may participate because he is paid to do so, because he derives psychological gratification from doing so, or even because he is coerced into it. But, if he is rational, he does not participate because of the benefits expected from a revolution. These benefits are public and available to all; rationally, then, there is no reason to participate to attain them.

If this conception of rationality is accepted, the area in which further investigation is needed concerns the nature of the psychological gratifications that might induce people to participate in revolutionary movements and the conditions under which these are likely to be perceived as positive benefits by large numbers of people. It is probably true that most participants in revolutionary movements obtain a certain amount of satisfaction from the very act of participating. The sense of comradeship and shared struggle in a worthwhile cause may well be perceived as benefits by many, if not all, participants. However, as it now stands, the inclusion of this factor serves to make the theory untestable. Furthermore, reliance on unspecified and unanalyzed psychological benefits to explain participation in revolutionary

---

[1]A second interesting result was not pursued here. A well-known theorem in the theory of public goods asserts that the supply of public goods is suboptimal. Translated, this roughly means that there are generally "too few" revolutions. This aspect was not pursued since it involves a technically more difficult literature and the application to revolutions poses some difficult problems.

movements is not very satisfactory. Revolutions are not constantly occurring, nor do they seem to be chance phenomena. Why, then, do people participate in revolutions at some times and not at others? If the answer to this question lies partly in the nature of the psychic gratification derived from participation in revolutionary movements, we need to know much more about this factor.

The answer to this kind of question might perhaps be obtained by examining the second basic participation hypothesis, proposed by Gurr. However, the task of developing this theory at the individual level and then integrating it with Olson's theory appears to be extremely difficult. The procedure would involve, in effect, an integration (or partial integration) of both of the participation hypotheses outlined above. So, we would have to develop a theory about the psychological factors that induce political rebellion and determine the conditions under which these will be strong enough to motivate people to join revolutionary movements on rational grounds.

If Gurr's theory included a good explanation of individual participation, this task would be greatly simplified. Unfortunately it does not. Gurr's theory rests on the eminently plausible notion that feelings of relative deprivation, under appropriate conditions, may be translated into political rebellion. This idea is probably a good starting point. But, the concept of relative deprivation suffers from a variety of problems that need to be solved before this basic idea can be developed into a good explanation. For example, before this idea can be usefully integrated into Olson's theory (or, for that matter, any other theory), we need to know how one can determine the level of relative deprivation experienced by a given individual and/or how this condition is related to other social conditions. To do this, we must first determine how people make social comparison or, to put the point technically: What constitutes a reference group for any individual in a given society? To my knowledge, this problem has not yet been solved.[2] Until it is, Gurr's theory and related efforts cannot explain why people rebel against the established political order. This means that such theories are not likely to solve the problems that stem from using Olson's theory to explain revolutions.

This does not mean, of course, that the attempt to refine psychological theories of rebellion should not be pursued, either for its own sake or to incorporate these into a rational-choice theory. Both Olson and Marx had problems in this area, indicating that psychological considerations are extremely important to explain individual rebellion. However, this problem is

---

[2]For an extended discussion of the relevance of reference groups to dissent, and the problems raised in this analysis, see John Urry, *Reference Groups and the Theory of Revolution* (London: Routledge & Kegan Paul, 1973).

complex and cannot be solved by anything as simple as a mechanical translation of Gurr's theory to the individual level.

One possible strategy here would be to retain Olson's rationality assumption and focus the psychological inquiry on the conditions under which large numbers of people are likely to experience such severe relative deprivation that they would rationally join revolutionary movements. This type of inquiry promises to be quite difficult. It does, however, serve to focus subsequent investigation. Furthermore, in view of the problems posed by Gurr's theory, it seems more feasible to retain some basic rational-choice orientation and try to incorporate psychological findings within it than to try to develop a theory of individual rebellion on the basis of psychological assumptions alone. In other words, judging from the theories I have examined, the most plausible hypothesis is that people act rationally when they join revolutionary movements, although psychological factors must be considered to explain their decision.

If psychological factors can be incorporated into Olson's theory successfully, this theory would provide a good explanation of individual rebellion. At this point, however, this has not been done, and the theory suffers from an inability to explain mass revolutions. This means that it is probably unwise to restrict inquiry solely to theories based on the conception of rationality assumed by Olson. There are different conceptions of rationality that may ultimately prove to be more successful as the bases of theories of revolution.

One of the greatest insights provided by Marxist theory is that principles of behavior—even of rational behavior—may change in differing social contexts. Marx's concept of man also assumed rationality. But, unlike Olson, Marx assumed that under certain conditions, people could engage in action that, if not rational from the point of view of the isolated, self-interested individual, would at least be rational from the perspective of the group as a whole. The assumption of such a transition is not unreasonable. Under many conditions, and particularly when public goods are involved, individuals, acting under Olson's conception of rationality, will end up in a worse position than class-conscious Marxist individuals. If people try to maximize their satisfaction, then, it is perfectly plausible to suppose they are capable of acting in the group interest, under certain conditions.

The Marxist account of this phenomenon, however, is not wholly satisfactory. Marx's notion that the transition from an individualist to a collectivist orientation takes place through shared struggles is interesting and should be pursued. Some evidence may be found supporting this view.[3] Further work in this area should indicate if Marx was correct in assuming that individuals will change principles of rational behavior in certain contexts.

---

[3] Abrahamson, *et al.*, "The Self or the Collectivity."

Beyond this, the broad outline of the rest of the Marxist account of participation in revolutionary movements is probably inaccurate. Judging from the experience of Western capitalist societies, it is not true that workers become socialist and initiate socialist revolutions. Perhaps Lenin was right in asserting that workers, "if left to their own devices," would only develop a trade-union consciousness.[4] At any rate, workers in the West have participated in trade-union struggles without becoming revolutionaries.

At this stage, it probably makes sense to try to determine if an individual's decision to participate in a revolutionary movement can be explained in terms of a rational choice, *given* his preferences, than to determine the actual nature of preferences of individuals in given social contexts. The two issues may, of course, be interdependent. Nevertheless, a focus on the rationality issue provides a starting point for research.

There are several ways this research could proceed. One line of investigation would be to use small group experiments to investigate conditions for collective revolt. There are, of course, many problems with extending the results of such studies to apply to revolutions, but the results of these studies should, nevertheless, indicate whether the Marxist conception of a learned group-oriented rationality has merit.

A second area of research would be to focus on a modified conception of individual rationality. While most people would probably argue that the behavior of all men at all times is not rational, in Olson's sense of the term, it seems reasonable to suppose that this type of rational consideration often enters into the decision-making process. The question then becomes to what extent these considerations affect the outcomes of decision processes. In other words, given that all choices may not be made on the basis of rational considerations alone, do cost and benefit considerations affect at least the probability that a decision will be made in a given direction?

The issue of the relevance of cost and benefit considerations to an individual's decision to participate in revolutionary movements might be investigated by applying the basic notions of the theory of public goods used by Olson to a conception of rationality based on stochastic choice models. The major purpose of this investigation would be to determine whether increased costs (benefits) would decrease (increase) the probability that an individual would participate in revolutionary movements. A well-developed theory of this sort might also help in determining how far participation in revolutions can be explained in terms of an individualistic rational choice.

The most likely explanation for revolutionary participation offered by the theories under consideration is that such participation occurs as the result of

---

[4]Lenin, "What Is To Be Done?" pp. 72–92.

a rational choice on the part of the participants. Whether such a choice can be explained solely in terms of the individualist conception of rationality, however, or whether this conception needs to be supplemented by more complex models of human choice behavior such as the one introduced by Marx remains unsolved. Once this issue is resolved, it may be possible to investigate more fully questions concerning the conditions under which large numbers of people are likely to adopt the type of preference structure that would make it rational for them to participate in revolutionary movements.

Explanations of the occurrence of revolutions in societies seem to be at an even more precarious stage. Several studies have indicated that certain factors are associated with political violence.[5] It is generally assumed that the same types of factors are associated with revolutions. These factors probably do not include all those that are relevant to revolutions. What makes the situation even more difficult is that in many cases there is conflicting evidence regarding the relevance of a factor and/or the nature of the relationship between it and political violence.

Consider, for example, the case of rapid economic growth. It might be argued that this factor would be accompanied by decreased violence since societies would then be equipped to satisfy "more wants." The general trend in the literature, however, is the converse argument: rapid socioeconomic change produces severe dislocations that result in increased instability.[6] The evidence is contradictory. Some studies found positive associations between political violence and rates of socioeconomic change.[7] Others found negative relationships between these two variables.[8] And at least one study indicates that the rate of economic change has little, if any, impact on either internal wars or more amorphous types of political violence.[9]

Similar results, if less dramatic, occur with other variables. Legitimacy, democracy, social cleavages, institutionalization, and regime coercive capability are some of the variables commonly thought to be relevant to political violence, in general, and revolutions, in particular. In all cases, however,

---

[5]For a list of the ones used by Gurr, see the Appendix.

[6]See, for example, Crane Brinton, *The Anatomy of Revolution* (New York: Vintage Books, 1965); Mancur Olson, Jr., "Rapid Growth as a Destabilizing Force," *Journal of Economic History,* 23:4 (December, 1963), pp. 529–59; and Pitirim Sorokin, *Social and Cultural Dynamics* (Boston: Horizon Books, 1957).

[7]Ivo Feierabend, *et al.,* "Social Change and Political Violence: Cross-National Patterns," in *Violence in America: Historical and Comparative Perspectives,* ed. by Hugh Graham and Ted Gurr (New York: Signet Books, 1969), p. 647; and Raymond Tanter and Manus Midlarsky, "A Theory of Revolution," *Journal of Conflict Resolution,* 11:3 (September, 1967), pp. 264–80.

[8]Douglas Bwy, "Political Instability in Latin America: The Cross-Cultural Test of a Causal Model," *Latin American Research Review,* 3:2 (Spring, 1968), pp. 17–66; and William H. Flanigan and Edwin Fogelman, "Patterns of Political Violence in Comparative Historical Perspective," *Comparative Politics,* 3:1 (October, 1970), pp. 1–20.

[9]Hibbs, *Mass Political Violence.*

although there is a common consensus that these factors are relevant, there is little evidence to indicate how important they are or how they affect political violence and revolutions. Studies in this area seem mainly to show that conclusions drawn are heavily dependent on the particular data base and/or particular measuring and statistical techniques used in the analysis. There is little reason to suppose that the results of one study can be accepted over the often conflicting findings of any other study.

This situation is not promising. It is one thing to believe that such things as socioeconomic change, regime coerciveness, and the like, must somehow be relevant to the occurrence of revolutions and quite another to get evidence to support this belief. At present, the cross-national study of the causes of political violence seems to be in such confusion that it is difficult to draw from it even the most tenuous conclusions about factors that are relevant to revolutions. It is, of course, possible to draw up a list of variables found to be correlated with revolutions or "internal wars." But, given conflicting evidence in the literature, it is difficult to decide if these correlations are spurious, artifacts of misleading statistical techniques, artifacts of extremely poor measuring devices, or genuine associations that may be used to construct more intricate theories of revolution.

The results of cross-national analyses provide evidence that is hardly conclusive; however, the functionalist and Marxist theories examined here do not take us much further. Johnson's theory is not sufficiently developed to provide an adequate explanation of revolutions. Without a specification of the system in terms of its components and the interrelationships among these—by using either structural or field descriptions—systems-analysis is poorly equipped to explain revolutions. As it stands, Johnson only develops a view of a basically harmonious social system that occasionally breaks down. Although it is probably true that revolutions only occur in societies that are somehow "not functioning adequately," the notion of a disequilibrated social system is so vague and covers such a multitude of sins that its value as a theoretical construct is minimal. Beyond a vague conceptualization of society and possibly some ill-defined "heuristic value," Johnson's theory contributes little to our understanding of revolutions.

Marx's theory fares somewhat better, if only because it provides a structurally more adequate explanation. Nevertheless, it is difficult to decide how far this theory takes us toward an understanding of revolutions.

Marx's theory is undoubtedly a simplification. Conflict among classes, for example, is not the only type of social conflict that occurs in societies, nor in many cases are class differences at the root of major social conflicts. This issue is not important. All theories simplify reality to some extent. The point is not whether all social conflict originates in class differences, but whether class conflict is an important enough source of the type of conflict leading to revolutions to provide an approximation to reality.

Judging from some of the "great revolutions," class conflict seems to play an important role in revolutions. In many, if not most, major revolutions there is sufficient polarization of interest along class lines to warrant the assertion of competing class claims. This does not mean, of course, that all workers support exactly the same program, or that some of the bourgeoisie will not support the proletarian class. It only means that most people support issues that, in broad terms, are similar to those supported by others of their class.

Although class conflict is undoubtedly an important factor in many revolutions, it has probably not played a major role in all events commonly designated as revolutions. It is difficult, for example, to portray the Cuban Revolution as a struggle between opposing classes. This does not mean that class conflict played no part in the Cuban Revolution. It means only that some of the major issues in this revolution do not seem to have been class oriented. In other words, it seems that class conflict is relevant to revolutions but is not the only type of conflict that leads to revolutions.

Furthermore, it is one thing to accept the importance of class conflict in revolutions and another to accept Marx's account of the nature and origins of such conflict. Judging from events in the United States and Western Europe, it does not seem to be the case that capitalist society creates the type of tensions that Marx believed would lead to a socialist revolution. There is, of course, class conflict in contemporary capitalist societies. But this conflict seems to be predominantly economic in nature, and has not led to significant polarization along class lines. In short, although class conflicts may be an important element of revolutions, the Marxist account does not adequately explain the origins and nature of such conflict.

If these theories are combined, we are left with a list of factors associated with revolutions. Such a list is hardly an outstanding contribution. It means, in effect, that we have some vague idea of what causes revolutions but we do not know how or why these factors produce revolutions. The situation is hardly very promising, but it is better than knowing nothing.

It is easy to conclude that none of the theories examined here provides an adequate explanation of revolutions. They do not, but that is beside the point. No general theory of revolutions, at this stage, can be expected to analyze all aspects of the revolutionary process in a completely adequate manner. The contribution these theories offer is that some of them are fully enough developed to pinpoint relatively specific areas that require further investigation. This is particularly true of the theories that rely on approaches with fairly restrictive underlying assumptions, that is, the theories proposed by Marx and Olson.

There is a variety of questions that might be further investigated within the general Marxist approach. An obvious point of attack would be to analyze why workers in advanced capitalist countries have not become socialist. This type of investigation could proceed in several ways, all of which have been studied to some extent by modern Marxist theoreticians. One possibility would be to focus on the general problem of consciousness and to try to determine whether there is any pattern to the emergence of human desires, related to social institutions. The work of the humanistic psychologists might be a useful start in this type of research.

A second possible "route" would be to hypothesize that Marx misjudged the extent to which the capitalist state is capable of internal transformation. An analysis of the types of changes that have taken place within capitalism during the past century might then be used to help explain the lack of severe class polarization in many capitalist countries.

A third, possibly related, focus stems from Lenin's theory of imperialism and its subsequent modification by other Marxist theoreticians.[10] This type of research would focus on the revolutionary implications of theories of imperialism. The aim here would be to formulate a theory of revolutions as an integral part of theories of imperialism.

These areas, of course, do not cover all (or even most) of the modifications of Marx's theory that might reasonably be attempted. They illustrate, however, the types of modifications that are possible. And, since these questions are narrower than the broad questions considered by Marx, it is just possible that research in these areas will ultimately yield enlightening results.

The rational-choice approach offers a similar variety of possible modifications. As has been indicated, psychological considerations might be incorporated into the model. Or, modified conceptions of rationality might be applied to the basic problem of choosing among alternative courses of action in situations in which public goods are involved. Again, what is important here is not the particular modifications that might be attempted, but simply that there are reasonably well defined avenues of investigation that can be pursued within the limits set by the approach.

The remaining two theories are, unfortunately, not as helpful in suggesting future research topics. Structural functionalism, of the type used by Johnson, is probably the least feasible approach to use in the near future. I will not argue here that functionalist explanations are not worthwhile. But it is very difficult to provide an adequate explanation of this type. To explain revolutions through the use of this variety of systems analysis, the investigator

---

[10]See above, pp. 118–21.

would have to specify essential variables, critical limits, other systemic variables, relevant environmental variables, parameters governing structural change, and either the mathematical structure of the system or some description of the system in terms of its fields. This presupposes a great amount of knowledge and/or speculation. Perhaps blind probes in this area might prove to be fruitful. At this point, however, such attempts would have to be "blind" since there is virtually no work that could be used to guide efforts in this direction.

The difficulty of using a structural-functional or systems approach in studying entire political systems suggests that this approach, if used at all, should be applied to a more restricted context. It may be possible to develop a mathematical structure that provides a reasonably good characterization of some aspect of the revolutionary process. For example, some type of systems analysis could conceivably be used to study the short-term or "proximate" causes of political rebellion. This could be used to study the intensity and duration of political rebellion in areas already experiencing some dgree of rebellion. The question of interest in this type of study would be: If political rebellion occurs in a society, what determines whether this rebellion is merely a minor incident or grows into a major protest movement, perhaps even of revolutionary proportions? This type of restricted question might be investigated within a systems perspective with some degiee of success. And, an adequate answer to this type of question would contribute significantly to our understanding of rebellion and revolution.

The final theory for consideration is Gurr's psychological perspective. The utility of this type of approach for the purposes of research on revolutions is particularly difficult to determine. As a psychological work, Gurr's theory is not good. It focuses on the wrong level of analysis, neglects considerations of interactions among individuals, and includes variables that have little, if anything, to do with frustration-aggression studies. Problems of this type might be investigated by changing the level of analysis or incorporating considerations of group psychology. Such efforts may be worthwhile. They provide, however, a rather nebulous area of investigation.

In addition to its psychological aspect, Gurr's theory may be considered from a different perspective. Basically, the work is a cross-national statistical analysis of political violence. In the sense that the term is being used here, this does not constitute an approach with specified assumptions. Nevertheless, it is an increasingly common technique that is used to study political violence and revolutions.

The basic idea behind the use of this technique is that factors relevant to revolutions and/or political violence may be found through the use of correlation and regression analysis. Once these factors are known, efforts will presumably be made to discover the various relationships among these factors. The final result would be a mathematical model of revolutions.

There is nothing wrong with this result, if it could be achieved. The question, however, is whether this attempt is likely to be successful if research proceeds in the direction indicated above. There are a variety of problems with the type of search techniques used in cross-national studies. Since no one is sure what variables to look for, different combinations of variables are used in different analyses. The particular variables deemed to be relevant are usually dependent on the other variables included in the analysis and/or the data base used. Furthermore, it is not feasible to include all of these different sets of variables in any single analysis since if this were done, the number of variables would approach (if not exceed) the number of cases. Consequently, the analyst is left in a situation in which a variable may or may not be relevant, depending on the other variables considered. Analysis is further complicated by the fact that parameter estimates vary widely from one data base to the next.

This situation would be difficult enough if the data used were sample data and principles of statistical inference could be invoked to reach conclusions about the population parameters. But the aggregate data used in cross-national studies do not constitute a random sample. Given messy results, it is extremely difficult to untangle the evidence without clear principles of inference.

Finally, the use of correlation or regression coefficients may not be a good test of relevancy. Mathematical models of revolutions may well involve non-linear relationships, and the use of a simple linear representation may result in the omission of certain variables that should actually be included.

Even if the above statistical problems were solved, still there would be the problem of determining whether variables included were spurious. This issue would pose no problem if the analysis were intended for the purposes of prediction. In terms of an explanatory account, however, the problem might become severe.

It is, of course, true that all types of analysis pose certain problems. I do not mean to imply here that cross-national studies should be abandoned as useless. Nevertheless, for the purpose of developing adequate explanations, such studies face severe limitations. As techniques of theory testing, they are probably as acceptable as anything else. As methods of theory construction, however, they leave much to be desired.

If the above considerations are accepted, the Marxist and rational-choice theories provide the most promising points of departure for subsequent research. This does not mean that research in these areas must lead to an adequate explanation of revolutions or that the other approaches considered will not ultimately prove to be better bases for theories of revolution. It simply means that at present the easiest and most feasible course of research lies in attempted modifications of either Marx, Olson, or both.

aPPenDIX[1]

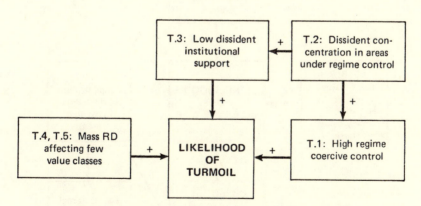

Figure 23. Conditions maximizing the likelihood of turmoil

---

[1]Diagrams from Ted Robert Gurr, *Why Men Rebel* (copyright © 1970 by Princeton University Press; Princeton Paperback, 1971): Figs. 16, p. 324, 18, p. 328, 20 p. 332, 23, p. 341, and 24 & 25, p. 342. Reprinted by permission of Princeton University Press.

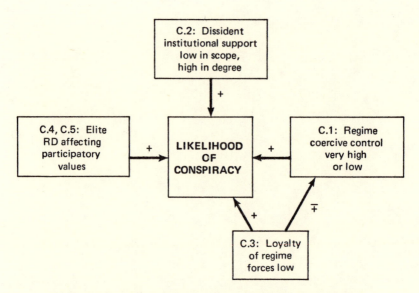

Figure 24. Conditions maximizing the likelihood of conspiracy

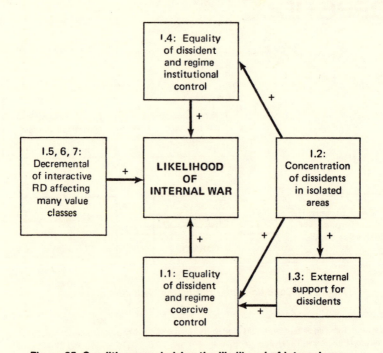

Figure 25. Conditions maximizing the likelihood of internal war

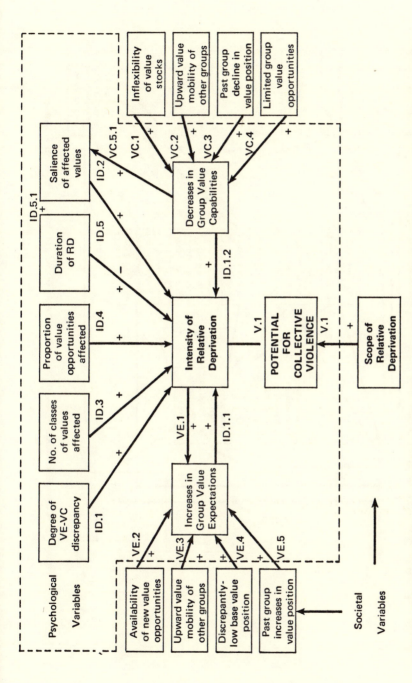

141

Figure 16. A complex causal model of the psychological and societal determinants of the potential for collective violence

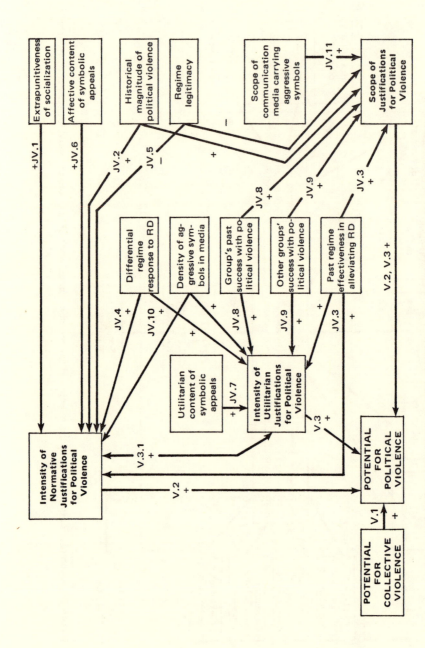

Figure 18. A complex causal model of the determinants of the potential for political violence

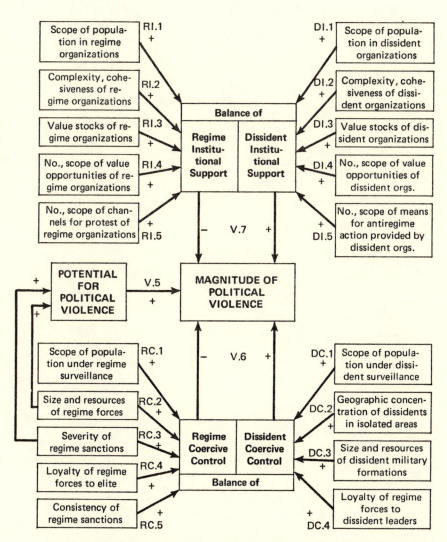

Figure 20. A causal model of the societal determinants of magnitude of political violence.

BIBLIOGRaPHY

Theories and Approaches

Achinstein, Peter and Stephen F. Barker, eds. *The Legacy of Logical Positivism.* Baltimore: Johns Hopkins Press, 1969.

Barker, Stephen F. *Induction and Hypothesis: A Study of the Logic of Confirmation.* Ithaca, N.Y.: Cornell University Press, 1957.

Borger, Robert and Frank Cioffi, eds. *Explanation in the Behavioral Sciences.* Cambridge: Cambridge University Press, 1970.

Braithwaite, R. B. *Scientific Explanation: A Study of the Function of Theory, Probability and Law in Science.* New York: Harper & Row, 1960.

Braybrooke, David. *Philosophical Problems of the Social Sciences.* New York: Macmillan, 1965.

Broadbeck, May, ed. *Readings in the Philosophy of the Social Sciences.* New York: Macmillan, 1968.

Brown, Robert. *Explanation in Social Science.* London: Routledge and Kegan Paul, 1963.

Daly, William T. *The Revolutionary: A Review and Synthesis.* Beverly Hills: Sage, 1972.

Emmet, Dorothy and Alasdair MacIntyre, eds. *Sociological Theory and Philosophical Analysis.* New York: Macmillan, 1970.

Freeman, Michael. "Review Article: Theories of Revolution," *British Journal of Political Science,* 2:3 (July, 1972), pp. 339–59.

Gardiner, Patrick. *The Nature of Historical Explanation.* London: Oxford University Press, 1952.

Hanson, Norwood. *Patterns of Discovery.* Cambridge: Cambridge University Press, 1958.

Hempel, Carl G. *Aspects of Scientific Explanation and Other Essays in the Philosophy of Science.* New York: The Free Press, 1970.

———. *Fundamentals of Concept Formation in Empirical Sciences.* Chicago: University of Chicago Press, 1952.

Hesse, Mary. *Models and Analogies in Science.* Notre Dame, Ind.: University of Notre Dame Press, 1966.

Kramnick, Isaac. "Reflections on Revolution: Definition and Explanation in Recent Scholarship," *History and Theory,* XI:1 (1972), pp. 26–63.

Kuhn, Thomas S. *The Structure of Scientific Revolutions.* Chicago: University of Chicago Press, 1962.

Landau, Martin. *Political Theory and Political Science.* New York: Macmillan, 1972.

MacIntyre, Alisdair. "Ideology, Social Science, and Revolution," *Comparative Politics,* 5:3 (April, 1973), pp. 321–42.

——— "Is a Science of Comparative Politics Possible?" in *Philosophy, Politics, and Society,* fourth series, ed. by Peter Laslett, W. G. Runciman, and Quentin Skinner. Oxford: Basil Blackwell, 1972, pp. 8–26.

Nagel, Ernest. *The Structure of Science.* New York: Harcourt, Brace and World, 1961.

Nardin, Terry. *Violence and the State: A Critique of Empirical Political Theory.* Beverly Hills: Sage, 1971.

Popper, Karl R. *Conjectures and Refutations: The Growth of Scientific Knowledge.* New York: Harper & Row, 1965.

———. *The Logic of Scientific Discovery.* New York: Harper & Row, 1968.

———. *Objective Knowledge: An Evolutionary Approach.* London: Oxford University Press, 1972.

Putnam, Hilary. "What Theories Are Not," in *Logic Methodology, and Philosophy of Science,* ed. by Ernest Nagel, Patrick Suppes, and Alfred Tarski. Stanford: Stanford University Press, 1962, pp. 240–51.

Quine, W. V. and J. S. Ullian. *The Web of Belief.* New York: Random House, 1970.

Rudner, Richard S. *Philosophy of Social Science.* Englewood Cliffs, N.J.: Prentice-Hall, 1966.

Russell, Bertrand. *Human Knowledge.* New York: Simon and Schuster, 1948.

Ryan, Alan, ed. *The Philosophy of Social Explanation.* London: Oxford University Press, 1973.

Salmon, Wesley C. *The Foundations of Scientific Inference.* Pittsburgh: University of Pittsburgh Press, 1967.

———. *Statistical Explanation and Statistical Relevance.* Pittsburgh: University of Pittsburgh Press, 1971.

Scheffler, Israel. *Science and Subjectivity.* New York: Bobbs-Merrill, 1967.

Scriven, Michael. "Explanations, Predictions, and Laws," in *Minnesota Studies in the*

Philosophy of Science, III, ed. by Herbert Feigel and Grover Maxwell. Minneapolis: University of Minnesota Press, 1962, pp. 170–230.

Smart, J. J. C. *Between Science and Philosophy.* New York: Random House, 1968.

Smokler, Howard. "Conflicting Conceptions of Confirmation," *The Journal of Philosophy,* LXV:9 (May, 1968), pp. 300–12.

Stone, Lawrence. "Theories of Revolution," *World Politics,* XVIII:2 (January, 1966), pp. 159–76.

Swinburne, R. G. "Choosing Between Confirmation Theories," *Philosophy of Science,* 37:4 (December, 1970), pp. 602–13.

Taylor, Daniel M. *Explanation and Meaning: An Introduction to Philosophy.* London: Cambridge University Press, 1970.

Winch, Peter. *The Idea of a Social Science.* New York: Humanities Press, 1958.

Wolin, Sheldon S. "The Politics of the Study of Revolution," *Comparative Politics,* 5:3 (April, 1973), pp. 343–58.

Rational Choice and Theories of Revolution

Arrow, Kenneth. "Exposition of the Theory of Choice Under Uncertainty," in *Decision and Organization,* ed. by C. B. McGuire and Roy Radner. Amsterdam: North-Holland Press, 1972, pp. 19–55.

Axelrod, Robert. *Conflict of Interest.* Chicago: Markham, 1970.

Barry, Brian M. *Sociologists, Economists and Democracy.* London: Collier-Macmillan Ltd., 1970.

Baumol, William J. "The Cardinal Utility Which Is Ordinal," *The Economic Journal,* LXVIII:272 (December, 1958), pp. 665–72.

———. *Welfare Economics and the Theory of the State,* 2nd ed. Cambridge: Harvard University Press, 1969.

Becker, Gary. "Irrational Behavior and Economic Theory," *The Journal of Political Economy,* LXX:1 (February, 1962), pp. 1–13.

Bonacich, Phillip. "Putting the Dilemma Back Into Prisoner's Dilemma," *The Journal of Conflict Resolution,* XIV:3 (September, 1970), pp. 379–87.

Breton, Albert. *The Economic Theory of Representative Government.* Chicago: Aldine, 1974.

———. "A Theory of the Demand for Public Goods," *Canadian Journal of Economics and Political Science,* 32 (1966), pp. 455–67.

——— and Raymond Breton. "An Economic Theory of Social Movements," *The American Economic Review,* 59:2 (May, 1969), pp. 198–205.

Buchanan, James. *Cost and Choice.* Chicago: Markham, n.d.

———. *The Demand and Supply of Public Goods.* Chicago: Rand McNally, 1968.

Burgess, Philip M. and James A. Robinson. "Alliances and the Theory of Collective Action: A Simulation of Coalition Processes," by *International Politics and Foreign Policy,* rev. ed., ed. by James N. Rosenau. New York: The Free Press, 1969, pp. 640–53.

Chamberlin, John. "Provision of Collective Goods as a Function of Group Size," *The American Political Science Review,* 68:2 (June, 1974), pp. 707–16.

Chamberlin, William Henry. *The Russian Revolution.* New York: Grosset & Dunlap, 1965.

Chipman, John S., Leonid Hurwicz, Marcel K. Richter and Hugo F. Sonnenschein, eds. *Preferences, Utility, and Demand.* New York: Harcourt Brace Jovanovich, 1971.

Coleman, James. "The Benefits of Coalition," *Public Choice,* VIII (Spring, 1970), pp. 45–61.

——. *The Mathematics of Collective Action.* Chicago: Aldine, 1973.

Davidson, Donald and Patrick Suppes in collaboration with Sidney Siegel. *Decision Making: An Experimental Approach.* Stanford: Stanford University Press, 1957.

Day, Richard H. "Rational Choice and Economic Behavior," *Theory and Decision,* 1:3 (March, 1971), pp. 229–51.

Dunn, John *Modern Revolutions.* Cambridge: Cambridge University Press, 1972.

Friedman, Milton and L. J. Savage. "The Expected-Utility Hypothesis and the Measurability of Utility," *The Journal of Political Economy,* LX:6 (December, 1952), pp. 463–74.

Forhlich, Norman, Joe Oppenheimer and Oran Young. *Political Leadership and Collective Goods.* Princeton: Princeton University Press, 1971.

Hardin, Russell. "Collective Action as an Agreeable n-Prisoners' Dilemma," *Behavioral Science,* 16:5 (September, 1971), pp. 472–81.

Harsanyi, John C. "Rational-Choice Models of Political Behavior vs. Functionalist and Conformist Theories," *World Politics,* 21:4 (July, 1969), pp. 513–38.

Head, John G. "Public Goods and Public Policy," *Public Finance,* 17:3 (1967), pp. 197–219.

—— and Carl S. Shoup. "Public Goods, Private Goods, and Ambiguous Goods," *The Economic Journal,* LXXIX:315 (September, 1969), pp. 567–72.

Hirschman, Albert O. *Exit, Voice, and Loyalty.* Cambridge: Harvard University Press, 1970.

Howard, Nigel. *Paradoxes of Rationality: Theory of Metagames and Political Behavior.* Cambridge: MIT Press, 1971.

Ireland, Thomas. "The Rationale of Revolt," *Papers on Non-Market Decision Making,* 3 (1967), pp. 49–66.

Kirchheimer, Otto. "Private Man and Society," *Political Science Quarterly,* 81 (March, 1966), pp. 1–24.

Kyburg, Jr., H. E. "Probability and Decision," *Philosophy of Science,* 33:3 (September, 1966), pp. 250–61.

Lave, Lester B. "Factors Affecting Cooperation in the Prisoner's Dilemma," *Behavioral Science,* 10 (January, 1965), pp. 26–38.

Leites, Nathan and Charles Wolf. *Rebellion and Authority: An Analytic Essay on Insurgency Conflicts.* Chicago: Markham, 1970.

Litvack, James M. and Wallace E. Oates. "Group Size and the Output of Public Goods," *Public Finance,* 25:1 (1970), pp. 42–58.

Luce, R. Duncan. *Individual Choice Behavior.* New York: Wiley, 1959.

—— and Howard Raiffa. *Games and Decisions.* New York: Wiley, 1957.

Mathiez, Albert. *The French Revolution.* New York: Grosset & Dunlap, 1964.

McKelvey, Richard D. and Peter C. Ordeshook. "A General Theory of the Calculus of Voting," in *Mathematical Applications in Political Science,* 6, ed. by James F. Herndon and Joseph L. Bernd. Charlottesville: University Press of Virginia, 1972, pp. 32–61.

Michalos, Alex C. "Postulates of Rational Preference," *Philosophy of Science,* XXXIV:1 (March, 1967), pp. 18–22.

Mishan, E. J. "The Relationship Between Joint Products, Collective Goods, and External Effects," *The Journal of Political Economy,* 77 (1969), pp. 329–48.

Moore, Jr., Barrington. *Social Origins of Dictatorship and Democracy.* Boston: Beacon Press, 1966.

Nieburg, H. L. *Political Violence.* New York: St. Martin's Press, 1969.

Ofshe, Lynne and Richard Ofshe. *Utility and Choice in Social Interaction.* Englewood Cliffs, N.J.: Prentice-Hall, 1970.

Olson, Jr., Mancur. "Economics, Sociology, and the Best of All Possible Worlds," *The Public Interest,* 12 (Summer, 1968), pp. 96–118.

———. *The Logic of Collective Action,* rev. ed. New York: Shocken Books, 1971.

——— and Richard Zeckhauser. "Collective Goods, Comparative Advantage, and Alliance Efficiency," in *Issues in Defense Economics,* ed. by Roland N. McKean. New York: Columbia University Press, 1967, pp. 25–63.

———. "An Economic Theory of Alliances," *The Review of Economics and Statistics,* 48:3 (August, 1966), pp. 266–79.

———. "The Efficient Production of External Economies," *The American Economic Review,* LX:3 (June, 1970), pp. 512–17.

Ozga, S. A. "Measurable Utility and Probability—A Simplified Rendering," *The Economic Journal,* LXVI:263 (September, 1956), pp. 419–30.

Pauly, Mark V. "Clubs, Commonality, and the Core: An Integration of Game Theory and the Theory of Public Goods," *Economica,* 34:136 (August, 1967), pp. 314–24.

Pruzan, Peter Mark. "Is Cost-Benefit Analysis Consistent With the Maximization of Expected Utility?" in *Operational Research and the Social Sciences,* ed. by J. R. Lawrence. London: Tavistock Publications, 1966, pp. 319–35.

Pryor, Frederic. *Public Expenditures in Communist and Capitalist Nations.* Homewood, Ill.: Richard D. Irwin, Inc., 1968.

Rapoport, Anatol and Albert Chammah. *Prisoner's Dilemma.* Ann Arbor: University of Michigan Press, 1965.

Riker, William H. and Peter C. Ordeshook. *An Introduction to Positive Political Theory.* Englewood Cliffs, N.J.: Prentice-Hall, 1973.

Rudé, George. *Revolutionary Europe.* New York: Harper & Row, 1964.

Russett, Bruce M. *What Price Vigilance?* New Haven: Yale University Press, 1970.

Salisbury, Robert. "An Exchange Theory of Interest Groups," *Midwest Journal of Political Science,* XIII:1 (February, 1969), pp. 1–32.

Samuelson, Paul A. "Contrast Between Welfare Conditions for Joint Supply and for Public Goods," *The Review of Economics and Statistics,* LI (1969), pp. 26–30.

———. "The Pure Theory of Public Expenditures," *The Review of Economics and Statistics,* XXXVI:4 (November, 1954), pp. 387–89.

———. "Utility, Preference, and Probability," in *The Collected Scientific Papers of Paul A. Samuelson,* vol. 1, ed. by Joseph Stiglitz. Cambridge: MIT Press, 1966, pp. 127–36.

Sen, Amartya. "Behavior and the Concept of Preference," *Economica,* 40 (August, 1973), pp. 241–59.

Shapiro, Michael J. "Rational Political Man: A Synthesis of Economic and Social-Psychological Perspectives," *The American Political Science Review,* LXIII:4 (December, 1969), pp. 1106–19.

Shubik, Martin. "Game Theory, Behavior, and the Paradox of the Prisoner's Dilemma: Three Solutions," *The Journal of Conflict Resolution,* XIV:2 (June, 1970), pp. 181–93.

Silver, Morris. "Political Revolution and Repression: An Economic Approach," *Public Choice,* XVII (Spring, 1974), pp. 63–71.

Simon, Herbert. "Theories of Bounded Rationality," in *Decision and Organization,* ed. by C. B. McGuire and Roy Radner. Amsterdam: North-Holland, 1972, pp. 161–76.

Tullock, Gordon. "A Model of Social Interaction," in *Mathematical Applications in Political Science,* 5, ed. by James F. Herndon and Joseph L. Bernd. Charlottesville: University Press of Virginia, 1971, pp. 4–28.

———. "The Paradox of Revolution," *Public Choice,* XI Fall, 1971), pp. 89–99.

———. *Private Wants, Public Means.* New York: Basic Books, 1970.

———. "Public Decisions as Public Goods," *The Journal of Political Economy,* 79:4 (July, 1971), pp. 913–18.

Ulam, Adam B. *The Bolsheviks.* New York: Collier, 1965.

Wagner, Richard E. "Pressure Groups and Political Entrepreneurs: A Review Article," *Papers on Non-market Decision Making,* 1 (1966), pp. 161–70.

Winch, David M. "Pareto, Public Goods and Politics," *Canadian Journal of Economics,* 2:4 (November, 1969), pp. 492–508.

The Psychology of Violence

Banks, Arthur. "Patterns of Domestic Conflict," *The Journal of Conflict Resolution,* XVI:1 (March, 1972), pp. 41–50.

Bateson, Gregory. "The Frustration-Aggression Hypothesis and Culture," *Psychological Review,* LXVIII:4 (July, 1941), pp. 350–55.

Bell, David. *Resistance and Revolution.* Boston: Houghton Mifflin, 1973.

Berkowitz, Leonard. *Aggression: A Social Psychological Analysis.* New York: McGraw-Hill, 1962.

———. "Frustrations, Comparisons, and Other Sources of Emotion Arousal as Contributors to Social Unrest," *The Journal of Social Issues,* 28:1 (1972), pp. 77–91.

———, ed. *Roots of Aggression.* New York: Atherton, 1969.

Bienen, Henry. *Violence and Social Change.* Chicago: University of Chicago Press, 1969.

Brinton, Crane. *The Anatomy of Revolution.* New York: Vintage, 1938.

Buss, Arnold. *The Psychology of Aggression.* New York: Wiley, 1962.

Bwy, Douglas. "Political Instability in Latin America: The Preliminary Test of a Causal Model," *Latin American Research Review,* III:2 (Spring, 1968), pp. 17–66.

Calvert, Peter. *A Study of Revolution.* Oxford: Clarendon Press, 1970.

Cantril, Hadley. *The Psychology of Social Movements.* New York: Wiley, 1941.

Church, Russell M. "The Varied Effects of Punishment on Behavior," *Psychological Review,* LXX (September, 1963), pp. 369–402.

Cohen, Arthur R. "Social Norms, Arbitrariness of Frustration, and Status of the Agent of Frustration in the Frustration-Aggression Hypothesis," *Journal of Abnormal and Social Psychology,* LI (1955), pp. 222–26.

Crawford, Thomas J. and Murray Naditch. "Relative Deprivation, Powerlessness, and Militancy: The Psychology of Social Protest," *Psychiatry* (May, 1970), pp. 208–23.

Davies, James C. "Political Stability and Instability: Some Manifestations and Causes," *Journal of Conflict Revolution,* XIII:1 (March, 1969), pp. 1–17.

———. "Toward a Theory of Revolution," *American Sociological Review,* XXVII (February, 1962), pp. 5–19.

Doob, Anthony and Lorraine Wood. "Catharsis and Aggression: Effects of Annoyance and Retaliation on Aggressive Behavior," *Journal of Personality and Social Psychology,* 22:2 (May, 1972), pp. 156–62.

Eckstein, Harry. "On the Etiology of Internal Wars," *History and Theory,* IV:2 (1965), pp. 133–63.

Fawcett, Jan, ed. *Dynamics of Violence.* Chicago: American Medical Association, 1972.

Feierabend, Ivo K. and Rosalind L. Frierabend. "Aggressive Behaviors Within Politics, 1948–1962: A Cross-National Study," *Journal of Conflict Resolution,* X:1 (September, 1966), pp. 249–71.

—— and Betty A. Nesvold. "The Comparative Study of Revolution and Violence," *Comparative Politics,* 5:3 (April, 1973), pp. 393–424.

——, Rosalind L. Feierabend and Ted Robert Gurr, eds. *Anger, Violence, and Politics.* Englewood Cliffs, N.J.: Prentice-Hall, 1972.

Fodor, Jerry A. *Psychological Explanation.* New York: Random House, 1968.

Geen, Russell and David Stonner. "Context Effects in Observed Violence," *Journal of Personality and Social Psychology,* 25:1 (January, 1973), pp. 145–50.

——. "Effects of Aggressiveness Habit Strength on Behavior in the Presence of Aggression-Related Stimuli," *Journal of Personality and Social Psychology,* 17:2 (February, 1971), pp. 149–53.

——. "Reactions to Aggression-Related Stimuli Following Reinforcement of Aggression," *The Journal of Psychology,* 83 (January, 1973), pp. 95–102.

Gentry, William. "Effects of Frustration, Attack, and Prior Aggressive Training on Overt Aggression and Vascular Processes," *Journal of Personality and Social Psychology,* 16:4 (December, 1970), pp. 718–25.

Geschwender, James A. "Explanations in the Theory of Social Movements and Revolutions," *Social Forces,* 47:2 (December, 1968), pp. 127–35.

Gillespie, John V. and Betty A. Nesvold, eds. *Macro-Quantitative Analysis.* Beverly Hills: Sage, 1971.

Graham, Hugh Davis and Ted Robert Gurr, eds. *Violence in America: Historical and Comparative Perspectives.* New York: Bantam, 1969.

Greene, Thomas H. *Comparative Revolutionary Movements.* Englewood Cliffs, N.J.: Prentice-Hall, 1974.

Grofman, Bernard and Edward Muller. The Strange Case of Relative Gratification and the Potential for Political Violence: The V-Curve Hypothesis. Papers presented at the 1972 Annual Meeting of the American Political Science Association.

Gurr, Ted Robert. "The Calculus of Civil Conflict," *The Journal of Social Issues,* 28:1 (1972), pp. 27–47.

——. "A Causal Model of Civil Strife: A Comparative Analysis Using New Indices," *American Political Science Review,* LXII:4 (December, 1968), pp. 1104–24.

——. "Psychological Factors in Civil Strife," *World Politics,* XX:2 (January, 1968), pp. 245–78.

——. "The Revolution-Social Change Nexus," *Comparative Politics,* 5:3 (April, 1973), pp. 359–92.

——. "Sources of Rebellion in Western Societies: Some Quantitative Evidence," *Annals of the American Academy of Political and Social Science,* 391 (September, 1970), pp. 128–44.

——. *Why Men Rebel.* Princeton: Princeton University Press, 1970.

—— and Raymond Duvall. Civil Conflict in the 1960's: A Reciprocal Theoretical

System with Parameter Estimates. Paper presented at the 1973 Annual Meeting of the International Studies Association.

Hamblin, Robert. "The Interference-Aggression Law," *Sociometry*, XXVI (June, 1963), pp. 190–216.

Hibbs, Jr.. Douglas A. *Mass Political Violence*. New York: Wiley, 1973.

Himmelweit, Hilde T. "Frustration and Aggression: A Review of Recent Experimental Work," in *Psychological Factors of Peace and War*, ed. by T. H. Pear. London: Hutchinson, 1950, pp. 159–91.

Hobsbawn, Eric J. *Primitive Rebels*. New York: Norton, 1965.

Knott, Paul and Bruce Drost. "Effects of Varying Intensity of Attack and Fear Arousal on the Intensity of Counter Aggression," *Journal of Personality*, 40:1 (March, 1972), pp. 27–37.

Kornhauser, William. *The Politics of Mass Society*. New York: The Free Press, 1959.

Kregarman, John and Philip Worchel. "Arbitrariness of Frustration and Aggression," *Journal of Abnormal and Social Psychology*, LXIII (July, 1961), pp. 183–87.

Larsen, Knud S., *et al.* "Is the Subject's Personality or the Experimental Situation a Better Predictor of a Subject's Willingness to Administer Shock to a Victim?" *Journal of Personality and Social Psychology*, 22:3 (June, 1972), pp. 287–95.

Leiden, Carl and Karl M. Schmidt. *The Politics of Violence: Revolution in the Modern World*. Englewood Cliffs, N.J.: Prentice-Hall, 1968.

Lupsha, Peter. "Explanations of Political Violence: Some Psychological Theories Versus Indignation," *Politics and Society*, 2:1 (Fall, 1971), pp. 89–104.

Maslow, A. H. "Deprivation, Threat, and Frustration," *Psychological Review*, XLVIII:4 (July, 1941), pp. 364–66.

Megargee, Edwin I. and Jack E. Hokanson, eds. *The Dynamics of Aggression*. New York: Harper & Row, 1970.

Miller, Neal *et al.* "The Frustration-Aggression Hypothesis," *Psychological Review*, XLVIII (July, 1941), pp. 337–42.

Morrison, Denton E. "Some Notes Toward a Theory of Relative Deprivation, Social Movements, and Social Change," *American Behavioral Scientist*, 14:5 (May–June, 1971), pp. 675–90.

Olson, Jr., Mancur. "Rapid Growth as a Destabilizing Force," *Journal of Economic History*, XXIII (December, 1963), pp. 529–52.

Pettee, George. *The Process of Revolution*. New York: Harper, 1938.

Rothaus, Paul and Philip Worchel. "The Inhibition of Aggression Under Nonarbitrary Frustration," *Journal of Personality*, XXVIII:1 (March, 1960), pp. 108–17.

Runciman, W. G. *Relative Deprivation and Social Justice*. Berkeley: University of California Press, 1966.

Russett, Bruce M. "Inequality and Instability: The Relation of Land Tenure to Politics," *World Politics*, XVI:3 (April, 1964), pp. 442–54.

Solnit, Albert J. "Aggression: A View of Theory Building in Psychoanalysis," *Journal of the American Psychoanalytic Association*, 20:3 (July, 1972), pp. 435–50.

Stokes, Donald. "Cross-Level Inferences as a Game Against Nature," in *Mathematical Applications in Political Science*, IV, ed. by Joseph Bernd. Charlottesville: University Press of Virginia, 1968, pp 62–83.

Tanter, Raymond and Manus Midlarsky. "A Theory of Revolution," *Journal of Conflict Resolution*, XI (September, 1967), pp. 264–80.

Toch, Hans. *Violent Men*. Chicago: Aldine, 1969.

Walter, E. V. *Terror and Resistance: A Study of Political Violence.* New York: Oxford University Press, 1969.

Wheeler, Ladd and Anthony R. Caggiula. "The Contagion of Aggression," *Journal of Experimental Social Psychology,* 2:1 (January, 1966), pp. 1–10.

Wolfenstein, E. Victor. *The Revolutionary Personality: Lenin, Trotsky, Gandhi.* Princeton: Princeton University Press. 1967.

Yates, Aubrey. *Frustration and Conflict.* New York: Wiley, 1962.

Revolution and the Social System

Ackhoff, Russell L. and Fred E. Emery. *On Purposeful Systems.* Chicago: Aldine, 1972.

Arendt, Hannah. *On Revolution.* New York: Viking, 1965.

Ashby, W. Ross. *Design for a Brain.* London: Chapman and Hall, 1960.

———. *An Introduction to Cybernetics.* London: University Paperbacks, 1964.

Buckley, Walter. *Sociology and Modern Systems Theory.* Englewood Cliffs, N.J.: Prentice-Hall, 1967.

———, ed. *Modern Systems Research for the Behavioral Scientist.* Chicago: Aldine, 1968.

Churchman, C. West. *The Design of Inquiring Systems.* New York: Basic Books, 1971.

———. *The Systems Approach.* New York: Delacorte Press, 1968.

Clark, Terry. Structural Functionalism, Exchange Theory, and the New Political Economy: Institutionalization as a Theoretical Linkage. Paper presented at the 1972 Annual Meeting of the Public Choice Society.

Coser, Lewis. *The Functions of Social Conflict.* New York: The Free Press, 1956.

Davies, James C. "The Circumstances and Causes of Revolution: A Review," *The Journal of Conflict Resolution,* XI:2 (June, 1967), pp. 247–57.

Demerath, III, N. J. and Richard A. Peterson, *System, Change, and Conflict.* New York: The Free Press, 1967.

Deutsch, Karl. *The Nerves of Government.* New York: The Free Press, 1966.

Downton, Jr., James V. *Rebel Leadership: Commitment and Charisma in the Revolutionary Process.* New York: The Free Press, 1973.

Durkheim, Emile. *Suicide.* New York: The Free Press, 1951.

Easton, David. *A Framework for Political Analysis.* Englewood Cliffs, N.J.: Prentice-Hall, 1965.

Eckstein, Harry, ed. *Internal War.* New York: The Free Press, 1964.

Eisinger, Peter K. "The Conditions of Protest Behavior in American Cities," *American Political Science Review,* LXVII:1 (March, 1973), pp. 11–28.

Emery, F. E., ed. *Systems Thinking.* Baltimore: Penguin, 1969.

Feierabend, Ivo K. *et al.* "Political Violence and Assassination: A Cross-National Assessment," in *Assassination and the Political Order,* ed. by William Brotty. New York: Harper & Row, 1971, pp. 54–140.

Firestone, Joseph and David McCormick. "An Exploration in Systems Analysis of Domestic Conflict," *General Systems Yearbook,* XVII (1972), pp. 79–120.

Flanigan, William and Edwin Fogelman. "Functional Analysis," in *Contemporary Political Analysis,* ed. by James C. Charlesworth. New York: The Free Press, 1967, pp. 72–85.

Forrester, Jay. "Counterintuitive Behavior of Social Systems," *Theory and Decision,* 2:2 (December, 1971), pp. 109–40.

Galtung, Johan. "A Structural Theory of Aggression," *Journal of Peace Research,* II (1964), pp. 95–119.

Gerlach, Luther. "Movements for Revolutionary Change: Some Structural Characteristics,'`American Behavioral Scientist,* 14:6 (July, 1971), pp. 812–36.

Gregor, A. James. "Political Science and the Uses of Functional Analysis," *American Political Science Review,* LXII:2 (June, 1968), pp. 425–39.

Grimm, Robert H. and Alfred F. McKay. *Society: Revolution and Reform.* Cleveland: Case Western Reserve Press, 1971.

Hajda, Jan. "A Reconceptualization of the Social System," *International Journal of Contemporary Sociology,* 9:1 (January, 1972), pp. 1–14.

Halpern, Manfred. "A Redefinition of the Revolutionary Situation," *Journal of International Affairs,* XXIII:1 (1969), pp. 54–75.

Hart, Thomas G. *The Dynamics of Revolution.* Ph.D. dissertation, University of Stockholm, 1971.

Hempel, Carl. "The Logic of Functional Analysis," in *Aspects of Scientific Explanation and Other Essays in the Philosophy of Science.* New York: The Free Press, 1970, pp. 297–330.

Holt, Robert T. "A Proposed Structural-Functional Framework," in *Contemporary Political Analysis,* ed. by James C. Charlesworth. New York: The Free Press, 1967, pp. 86–107.

Huntington, Samuel P. *Political Order in Changing Societies.* New Haven: Yale University Press, 1968.

Isajiw, Wsevalod. *Causation and Functionalism in Sociology.* London: Routledge and Kegan Paul, 1968.

Johnson, Chalmers. *Revolutionary Change.* Boston: Little, Brown, 1966.

Kirchheimer, Otto. "Conflicting Conditions and Revolutionary Breakthrough," *American Political Science Review,* LIX:4 (December, 1965), pp. 964–74.

Knight, Douglas E., Huntington, W. Curtis and Lawrence J. Fogel, eds. *Cybernetics, Simulation, and Conflict Resolution.* New York: Spartan Books, 1971.

Lazlo, Ervin. *Introduction to Systems Philosophy.* New York: Gordon and Breach, 1972.

Levy, Marion. *The Structure of Society.* Princeton: Princeton University Press, 1950.

Martindale, Don, ed. *Functionalism in the Social Sciences.* Philadelphia: The American Academy of Political and Social Science, 1965.

McClelland, Charles A. "Systems Theory and Human Conflict," in *The Nature of Human Conflict,* ed. by Elton B. McNeil. Englewood Cliffs, N.J.: Prentice-Hall, 1965, pp. 250–73.

Merton, Robert K. *Social Theory and Social Structure.* Glencoe, Ill.: The Free Press, 1957.

Midlarsky, Manus. "Mathematical Models of Instability and a Theory of Diffusion," *International Studies Quarterly,* 14:1 (March, 1970), pp. 60–84.

Nilson, Sten Sparre. "Measurement and Models in the Study of Stability," *World Politics,* XX:1 (October, 1967), pp. 1–29.

Parsons, Talcott. *The Social System.* New York: The Free Press, 1964.

Piaget, Jean. *Structuralism.* New York: Basic Books, 1970.

Rapoport, Anatol. "Modern Systems Theory—An Outlook for Coping with Change," *General Systems Yearbook,* XV (1970), pp. 15–25.

Revans, R. W. "The Structure of Disorder," in *Survey of Cybernetics,* ed. by J. Rose. London: Iliffe Books, 1969, pp. 331–45.

Rummel, Rudolph. "A Field Theory of Social Action with Application to Conflict Within Nations," *General Systems Yearbook,* X (1965), pp. 183–211.

Simmel, Georg. *Conflict.* Glencoe, Ill.: The Free Press, 1955.

Simon, Herbert. *The Sciences of the Artificial.* Cambridge: MIT Press, 1969.

Smelser, Neil. *Theory of Collective Behavior.* New York: The Free Press, 1962.

Southwood, Ken. "Riot and Revolt: Sociological Theories of Political Violence," *Peace Research Reviews,* 1:3 (June, 1967).

Stephens, Jerome. "The Logic of Functional and Systems Analyses in Political Science," *Midwest Journal of Political Science,* XIII:2 (May, 1969), pp. 367–94.

Taylor, Alastair M. "For Philosophers and Scientists: A General Systems Paradigm," *International Philosophical Quarterly,* XIII:1 (March, 1973), pp. 111–29.

Tilly, Charles. "Does Modernization Breed Revolution?" *Comparative Politics,* 5:3 (April, 1973), pp. 425–47.

———. *The Vendée: A Sociological Analysis of the Counter-revolution of 1793.* Cambridge: Harvard University Press, 1964.

Timasheff, Nicholas S. *War and Revolution.* New York: Sheed and Ward, 1965.

Vickers, Geoffrey. "A Classification of Systems,"*General Systems Yearbook,* XV (1970), pp. 3–6.

Von Bertalanffy, Ludwig. *General System Theory.* New York: George Braziller, 1968.

Von Foerster, Heinz and George W. Zopf, Jr., eds. *Principles of Self-Organization.* Oxford: Pergamon Press, 1962.

Wright, Larry. "Explanation and Teleology," *Philosophy of Science,* 39:2 (June, 1972), pp. 204–18.

Zagorim, Perez. "Theories of Revolution in Contemporary Historiography," *Political Science Quarterly, LXXXVIII:1 (March, 1973), pp. 23–52.*

The Marxist Theory of Revolutions

Abrahamson, Mark *et al.* "The Self or the Collectivity: Simulation of a Marxian Hypothesis." *Social Forces,* 47:3 (March, 1969), pp. 299–305.

Addis, Laird. "Freedom and the Marxist Philosophy of History," *Philosophy of Science,* 33:2 (June, 1966), pp. 101–17.

Althusser, Louis. *For Marx.* New York: Random House, 1969.

Avineri, Shlomo. *The Social and Political Thought of Karl Marx.* Cambridge: Cambridge University Press, 1971.

———, ed. *Marx's Socialism.* New York: Lieber-Atherton, 1973.

Balbus, Isaac D. "The Concept of Interest in Pluralist and Marxian Analysis," *Politics and Society,* 1:2 (February, 1971), pp. 151–77.

Berger, Peter and Thomas Luckmann. *The Social Construction of Reality.* Garden City, N.Y.: Doubleday, 1966.

Bober, M. M. *Karl Marx's Interpretation of History.* New York: Norton, 1965.

Boh, Ivan. "Marxist Dialectic and Formal Logic," *Proceedings of the American Catholic Philosophical Association,* XL (1966), pp. 77–85.

Cherry, Robert. "Class Struggle and the Nature of the Working Class," *The Review of Radical Political Economics,* V:2 (Summer, 1973), pp. 47–86.

Christman, Henry M., ed. *Essential Works of Lenin.* New York: Bantam, 1966.

Easton, Lloyd D. "Alienation and Empiricism in Marx's Thought," *Social Research,* 37:3 (Autumn, 1970), pp. 402–27.

Fleischer, Helmut. *Marxism and History.* New York: Harper & Row, 1973.

Friedman, Daniel J. "Marx's Perspective on Objective Class Structure," *Polity,* VI:3 (Spring, 1974), pp. 318–44.

Gintis, Herbert. "Alienation and Power," *The Review of Radical Political Economics,* 4:5 (Fall, 1972), pp. 1–34.

Glass, James M. "Marx, Kafka and Jung: The Appearance of Species-Being," *Politics and Society,* 2:2 (Winter, 1972), pp. 255–71.

Gorz, Andre. *Socialism and Revolution.* Garden City, N.Y.: Anchor Books, 1973.

Gramsci, Antonio. *Selections from the Prison Notebooks,* ed. by Quintin Hoare and Goffrey Nowell Smith. New York: International Publishers, 1971.

Habermas, Jurgen. *Knowledge and Human Interests.* Boston: Beacon Press, 1971.

Hammen, Oscar. "Alienation, Communism, and Revolution in the Marx-Engels Brief-wechsel," *Journal of the History of Ideas,* 33 (January–March, 1972), pp. 77–100.

Harris, John. "The Marxist Conception of Violence," *Philosophy and Public Affairs,* 3:2 (Winter, 1974), pp. 192–220.

Haupt, Heinz-Gerhard and Stephen Leibfried. "Marxism Analysis of Politics or Theory of Social Change?: Toward a Marxian Theory of the Political Domain," *Politics and Society,* 3:1 (Fall, 1972), pp. 33–47.

Hegel, G. W. F. *Reason in History.* Indianapolis: Bobbs-Merrill, 1953.

Hodges, Donald Clark. "Marx's Concept of Egoistic Man," *Praxis,* 4:3–4 (1968), pp. 364–75.

Hook, Sidney. "Dialectic in Society and History," in *Readings in the Philosophy of Science,* ed. by Herbert Feigl and May Brodbeck. New York: Appleton-Century-Crofts, 1953, pp. 701–13.

Horkheimer, Max. *Critical Theory.* New York: Herder and Herder, 1972.

Jay, Martin. *The Dialectical Imagination.* Boston: Little, Brown, 1973.

Kirchheimer, Otto. "Marxism, Dictatorship, and the Organization of the Proletariat," in *Politics, Law, and Social Change,* ed. by Frederic S. Burin and Kurt L. Shell. New York: Columbia University Press, 1969, pp. 22–32.

Korsch, Karl. *Marxism and Philosophy.* New York: Monthly Review Press, 1970.

Lichtheim, George. *From Marx to Hegel.* New York: Seabury Press, 1974.

——. *Marxism: An Historical and Critical Study.* New York: Praeger, 1965.

Lubasz, Heinz. "Marx's Conception of the Revolutionary Proletariat," *Praxis,* 5:1–2 (1969), pp. 288–90.

Lukács, Georg. *History and Class Consciousness.* Cambridge: MIT Press, 1971.

Magri, Lucio. "Problems of the Marxist Theory of the Revolutionary Party, *New Left Review,* 10 (March–April, 1970), pp. 97–128.

Malecki, Edward S. "Theories of Revolution and Industrialized Societies," *The Journal of Politics,* 35:4 (November, 1973), pp. 948–85.

Mandel, Ernest. *Marxist Economic Theory,* 2 vols. New York: Monthly Review Press, 1970.

Marcuse, Herbert. *Reason and Revolution.* Boston: Beacon Press, 1960.

——. "Re-examination of the Concept of Revolution," *Diogenes,* 64 (Winter, 1968), pp. 17–26.

——. *Studies in Critical Philosophy.* Boston: Beacon Press, 1972.

Marković, Mihailo. "The Concept of Revolution," *Praxis,* 5:1–2 (1969), pp. 41–54.

Marx, Karl. *Capital,* 3 vol., ed. by Frederick Engels. New York: International Publishers, 1967.

————. *On Colonialism and Modernization,* ed. by Shlomo Alvineri. New York: Doubleday, 1969.

————. *Early Writings,* ed. by T. B. Bottomore. New York: McGraw-Hill, 1963.

————. *The Economic and Philosophic Manuscripts of 1844,* ed. by Dirk J. Struik. New York: International Publishers, 1964.

————. *Grundrisse.* New York: Vintage Books, 1973.

————. *On Revolution,* ed. by Saul K. Padover. New York: McGraw-Hill, 1971.

————. *Revolution and Counter Revolution,* ed. by Eleanor Mary Aveling. New York: Capricorn Books, 1971.

———— and Frederick Engels. *The German Ideology.* New York: International Publishers, 1963.

————. *Ireland and the Irish Question,* ed. by R. Dixon. New York: International Publishers, 1972.

————. *Selected Works.* New York: International Publishers, 1968.

Mattick, Paul. *Marx and Keynes: The Limits of the Mixed Economy.* Boston: Extending Horizons Books, 1969.

McLellan, David. "Marx's View of the Unalienated Society," *The Review of Politics,* 31:4 (October, 1969), pp. 459–65.

————. *The Thought of Karl Marx.* London: Macmillan, 1971.

Mészáros, István. *Marx's Theory of Alienation.* New York: Harper & Row, 1970.

Moore, Stanley. "Marx and the Origin of Dialectical Materialism," *Inquiry* 14:4 (Winter, 1971), pp. 420–29.

Novack, George. *An Introduction to the Logic of Marxism.* New York: Pathfinder Press, 1971.

Ollman, Bertell. *Alienation: Marx's Conception of Main in Capitalist Society.* Cambridge: Cambridge University Press, 1971.

————. "Toward Class Consciousness Next Time: Marx and the Working Class," *Politics and Society,* 3:1 (Fall, 1972), pp. 1–24.

Ossowski, Stanislaw. *Class Structure in the Social Consciousness.* New York: The Free Press, 1963.

Petrovic, Gajo. "Dialectical Materialism and the Philosophy of Praxis," *Boston Studies in the Philosophy of Science,* IV. Holland: D. Reidel Publishing Co., 1969, pp. 261–76.

Piccone, Paul. "Phenomenological Marxism," *Newsletter on Comparative Studies of Communism,* V:2 (February, 1972), pp. 23–59.

Plamenatz, John. *German Marxism and Russian Communism.* London: Longmans, Green, 1954.

————. *Man and Society,* vol. 2. New York: McGraw-Hill, 1963.

Plekhanov, George. *The Materialist Conception of History.* New York: International Publishers, 1940.

————. *The Role of the Individual in History.* New York: International Publishers, 1940.

Popper, Karl R. *The Open Society and Its Enemies,* vol. 2. Princeton: Princeton University Press, 1966.

Portes, Alejandro. "On The Interpretation of Class Consciousness," *American Journal of Sociology,* 77:2 (September, 1971), pp. 228–44.

Przeworski, Adam and Glaucio A. D. Soares. "Theories in Search of a Curve: A Contextual Interpretation of Left Vote," *American Political Science Review,* LXV:1 (March, 1971), pp. 51–68.

Reich, Wilhelm. "What Is Class Consciousness?" *Liberation,* 16:5 (October, 1971), pp. 15–19.

Schram, Stuart R. *The Political Thought of Mao Tse-tung,* rev. ed. New York: Praeger, 1969.

Schroyer, Trent. "Marx's Theory of the Crisis," *Telos,* 14 (Winter, 1972), pp. 106–25.

Sweezy, Paul M. *The Theory of Capitalist Development.* New York: Oxford University Press, 1942.

—————. "The Transition to Socialism," *Monthly Review,* 23:1 (May, 1971), pp. 1–16.

Walpe, Harold. "The Problem of the Development of Revolutionary Consciousness," *Telos,* 4 (Fall, 1969), pp. 113–44.

Wolfe, Alan. "New Directions in the Marxist Theory of the State," Paper presented at the 1973 Annual Meeting of the American Political Science Association.

Zeitlin, Irving. *Marxism: A Re-examination.* Princeton: Van Nostrand, 1967.

InDex

Contradictions *(cont'd)*
  defined, 101
Cuban Revolution, 60n, 92, 134

Daniels, Robert, 2n
Davidson, Donald, 32n
Davies, James, 57n, 63n, 70n
Debray, Regis, 112n
Definitions
  problems of, 19–20
  theoretical relevance of, 7–8
Disequilibrium, 78–81, 87, 90–91, 133
Dissynchronization, 20, 79
Dollard, John, 57n
Drost, Bruce, 58n
Duvall, Raymond, 72n

Easton, David, 5n, 11n, 84n, 90n
Economic crises, 103–105, 115–116, 121
Elite intransigence, 79–81, 88–92
Essential variables
  (See Functional prerequisites)

Falling tendence of the rate of profit,
  102–104, 115
Feierabend, Ivo, 57n, 132n
Feierabend, Rosalind, 57n
Flanigan, William, 132n
Fleischer, Helmut, 98n
Fogelman, Edwin, 132n
Freeman, Michael, 3n, 59, 59n, 60n, 72,
  72n, 80n
French Revolution, 6–7, 45–47, 60n, 92
Friedman, Daniel, 105n, 108n
Friedman, Milton, 30n, 33n
Frohlich, Norman, 38n
Frustration-aggression hypothesis, 12n,
  51, 57–59, 62, 64, 66, 66n, 67–68
Functional prerequisites, 77–78, 83–86,
  136
Functionalism
  (See Structural functionalism)

Game theory, 38–41
Geen, Russell, 58n
General Systems Theory, 76, 96
Gentry, William, 57n
Gramsci, Antonio, 112n
Gregor, A. James, 76n
Gurr, Ted Robert, 3, 3n, 4, 12, 50–74, 76,
  87, 125, 127–130, 136, 139–143

Hardin, Russel, 39n, 41n
Head, John, 25n
Hempel, Carl, 7n, 16n, 77n
Hibbs, Douglas, Jr., 2n, 72n, 132n
Homeostatic systems, 11, 77–78, 82, 84

Imperialism, 115, 118–121, 135

Increasing misery of workers, 103–105,
  116–117, 120n
Ireland, Thomas, 34, 34n, 44n

Johnson, Chalmers, 3, 3n, 5, 75–96, 126
  133, 136

Kirchheimer, Otto, 48n
Knott, Paul, 58n
Kramnick, Isaac, 3n, 89, 89n
Kyburg, H. E., Jr., 30n

Lakatos, Imre, 8n, 18n
Landau, Martin, 77n
Leadership, 37–40, 112–113, 122
Legitimacy, 20, 55, 67, 79, 132
Lenin, 27, 112, 112n, 118n, 131n, 135
Lichtheim, George, 101n
Luce, R. Duncan, 41n
Luckmann, Thomas, 108n
Lupsha, Peter, 63n

McKelvey, Richard, 42n
McLellan, David, 120n
Mandel, Ernest, 103n, 118n
Mao Tse-tung, 27
Marcuse, Herbert, 113n
Marschak, J., 32n
Marx, Karl, 3, 3n, 5, 12, 76, 94, 94n,
  96–123, 127–132, 134–135, 138
Mathiez, Albert, 2n
Mattick, Paul, 105n
Methodological individualism, 64
Mexican Revolution, 7
Michalos, Alex, 30n
Midlarsky, Manus, 132n
Moore, Barrington, Jr., 2n
Moore, Stanley, 98n
Morris, Bernard, 119n

Nagel, Ernest, 13n, 16n, 78n
Nardin, Terry 3n
Nesvold, Betty, 60, 60n
Nie, Norman, 65n

Oberschall, Anthony, 48n
Ofshe, Lynne, 32n
Ofshe, Richard 32n
Ollman, Bertell, 107n, 112n
Olson, Mancur, Jr., 3, 3n, 4, 11, 23–49,
  76, 95, 110, 125, 127–131, 132n 135,
  138
Oppenheimer, Joe, 38n
Ordeshook, Peter, 9n, 42n
Organic composition of capital, 103,
  103n, 115

Petrović, Gajo, 98n
Plamenatz, John, 100, 100n

Political violence
    correlates of, 132
    forms of, 52–53, 56, 59–60
    justifications for, 55, 72
    magnitude of, 52–53, 55–56, 71–72
    potential for, 54–55, 72
Portes, Alejandro, 114n
Powell, G. Bingham, Jr., 65n
Precipitating factors
    (*See* Accelerators)
Prewitt, Kenneth, 65n
Productive forces, 99–101
Pruzan, Peter Mark, 31n
Pryor, Frederick, 28n
Przeworski, Adam, 114n
Public goods, 11, 25–26, 136

Raiffa, Howard, 41n
Rapoport, Anatol, 41n
Rationality
    defined, 25, 29–33
    in revolutionary movements, 11, 24,
        47, 50, 128, 130–132
Reference groups, 61–62, 129
Relations of production, 99–101
Relative deprivation, 51, 53–54, 56,
    61–63, 67, 70, 129
Riker, William, 9n
Robinson, James, 28n
Rothaus, Paul, 58n
Rudner, Richard, 77n
Rummel, Rudolph, 53n, 60, 60n
Russett, Bruce, 28n
Russian Revolution, 6–7, 14, 45–47, 92

Salmon, Wesley, 14, 14n, 15, 15n, 16,
    17n
Samuelson, Paul, 33n
Savage, L. J., 30n
Selective incentives, 27, 35, 38, 49, 67,
    128
Sen, Amartya, 30n
Shubik, Martin, 41n
Silver, Morris, 34, 34n
Smelser, Neil, 3n, 93, 93n
Soares, Glaucio A. D., 114n
Sorokin, Pitirim, 132n

Spurious correlation, 15–16, 52, 66, 68,
    73–74, 90, 126, 133
Statistical relevance, 14
Stephens, Jerome, 77n
Stokes, Donald, 65n
Stone, Lawrence, 3n, 89n
Stonner, David, 58n
Structural change, 5–7, 79, 85, 87–88,
    101, 136
Structural-functionalism, 5, 76, 78, 136
Suppes, Patrick, 32n
Surplus value, 103, 103n
Sweezy, Paul, 102n, 103n, 118n
System stability, 77–78

Tanter, Raymond, 60, 60n, 132n
Taylor, Daniel, 13n
Terkel, Studs, 117n
Theories
    assumptions, 8–11, 25, 31–33,
        76–77, 96, 115
    confirmation of, 17–19
    explanation of, 13–17, 21
    hypotheses, 9, 18
    revision of, 9
Trade union consciousness, 111–113,
    117, 122, 127, 131
Tullock, Gordon, 34, 34n, 36n

Ultrastable systems, 83–85, 87, 90
Urry, John, 129n
Utility, maximization of, 30–31, 67

Van Ypersele de Strihou, Jacques, 28n
Von Bertalanffy, Ludwig, 76n

Wise, John, 32n
Wolfe, Alan, 98n
Wolfenstein, E. Victor, 3n
Wonnacott, Ronald, 72n
Wonnacott, Thomas, 72n
Worchel, Philip, 58n

Yotopoulos, Pan, 32n
Young, Oran, 38n

Zeckhauser, Richard, 28n